THE NAVAL BRIGADE
IN SOUTH AFRICA.

LONDON:
GILBERT AND RIVINGTON, PRINTERS,
ST. JOHN'S SQUARE.

FORT EKOWI. Y. LAND.

THE

NAVAL BRIGADE

IN

SOUTH AFRICA

DURING THE YEARS 1877—78—79.

BY

FLEET-SURGEON HENRY F. NORBURY, C.B., R.N.,

LATE OF H.M. FLAG-SHIP "ACTIVE,"
AND PRINCIPAL MEDICAL OFFICER OF THE NAVAL FORCES LANDED IN
SOUTH AFRICA,
OF COLONEL PEARSON'S COLUMN, OF FORT EKOWE, ETC.

London:
SAMPSON LOW, MARSTON, SEARLE, & RIVINGTON,
CROWN BUILDINGS, 188, FLEET STREET.
1880.

[All rights reserved.]

TO MY COMRADES

OF THE

NAVAL BRIGADE,

LATELY SERVING IN SOUTH AFRICA, THIS VOLUME

IS INSCRIBED.

PREFACE.

In publishing this volume, I think that some explanation is necessary as to my reasons for doing so. In the first place, because I am aware that books on South Africa are already "thick as leaves in Vallambrosa;" and, secondly, because, when a man wishes to find an excuse for inflicting his compositions on the public, he frequently, sometimes archly, says that he "does so at the request of numerous friends:" this is, however, really and precisely what I am doing in the present instance—my friends of the Naval Brigade of H.M.S. "Active" having repeatedly requested me to write an account of our campaigns, and I think principally from the fact that on both occasions I kept a rather extensive journal of our proceedings. The matter contained in the following pages is either such as came under my personal observation, or such as was imparted to me by those who, from long residence, had become thoroughly conversant with Kafir life. To my friend the Rev. Mr. Robertson, of Kwamagwaza, Zululand, I am chiefly indebted for what I know of the rise, progress, habits, and customs of the Zulu nation; and I shall always look back with pleasure to that eventful time, when his interesting lectures and conversations were the only bright spots in a very gloomy scene. In compiling this volume I have consulted no published work whatever, with the exception of Dohne's Zulu-Kafir Dictionary, to which I had recourse when in doubt as to the meaning of Kafir terms. I am fully aware both of the defects and shortcomings of this work; but should I have succeeded in furnishing my old comrades of the Naval Brigade, now scattered far and wide, with an acceptable record of those, to us, memorable times in South Africa, I shall consider that my object has been fully attained.

Simon's Town, Cape of Good Hope.
April, 1880.

TERMS COMMONLY USED IN KAFFRARIA.

Kloof	Valley, or large ravine.
Vley	Pond.
Krantz	Precipice.
Veldt	An open grassy country.
Kraal	Cattle enclosure, generally with the huts surrounding it. A village.
Kop, or Kopje	Head, or headland.
Sluit	Rivulet.
Reim	Raw-hide tether.
Laager	Camp of refuge.
Drift	A ford.
Trek	Journey.
Span	A team, usually of oxen.
Outspan	Unyoke the oxen.
Mealies	Maize.
Sjambok	Whip of hide.
Vorlupen	Leader of an ox span.
Kaross	A rug made of skins.
Spoor	A track.
Biltung	Sun-dried meat.

THE KAFIR TRIBES.

CUSTOMS AND HABITS OF THE KAFIR TRIBES.

ALTHOUGH the campaign of 1877-78 against the Gaika and Galeka tribes is generally spoken of as the Kafir War, yet the term Kafir, as commonly employed, is of far more general application, and includes all the numerous black tribes which occupy Southern Africa from the eastern parts of the Cape Colony to the Portuguese settlement at Delagoa Bay. There is some dispute as to the precise origin of the term, but it is generally regarded as of Arabic extraction, and signifies an unbeliever or infidel, and it was probably first applied to them by those Mohammedans who, before the advent of the Portuguese, traded along the coasts. It is almost unnecessary to state that none of the South African tribes would recognize themselves by such a name, but that every one rejoices in its individual patronymic, such as Xosa, Tembu, Pondo, Bomvana, Zulu, &c. It is generally agreed that the majority of these tribes are branches of a common trunk; the principal ones, at least, speak dialects of the same language, the vocabularies of the Zulu, Xosa, and Tembu in particular possessing great similarity; but modified by intercourse with foreigners, English, Dutch, Arabs, and Portuguese, their language includes many hybrid words, that of the Xosa the most so, that of the Zulu the least. It abounds in clicks, of which there are three principal ones, and there is great stress laid on certain syllables, which are also lengthened exceedingly, so as to give them a drawling sound. The plural of many nouns is formed by their combination with Ama, which is also used as a prefix to signify a race or nation, as Amaxosa, Amapondo. The appellations of these tribes and of their subdivisions are, as a rule, derived either from an ancestor, as Galeka, Gaika, Xosa, which again often originate in some act of that ancestor, as in the latter instance, Xosa signifying, "One who has broken away from his people," or else from some peculiarity of the tribe itself, thus: Pondo, "possessing horns," Tembu, "a polygamist," and Zulu, "a wanderer." There are two accounts of the rise of another tribe, with which this narrative will bring us into more intimate association, viz., the Fingoes: one being, that they were originally made prisoners by the Xosa in a war with a northern race, reduced to slavery, and regarded as dogs, whence the name Fingo, being fed in a similar manner by having thrown to them the leavings of their masters: the other, that they were dispersed tribes, driven from the north, probably by the Zulus under Chaka, that they wandered into the Galeka country, demanding refuge, and using a word "Fengusa" to express their want. The Kafirs were ignorant of its signification, but subsequently, having converted them into slaves, they retained it as their name. Some of the Fingoes call themselves Xlubi.

The Kafirs reside in collections of huts, known as Kraals, although this word strictly is applied to the circular fold or enclosure in which cattle are confined at night, and outside which is a ring of huts. These huts are acpacious, formed of wattle-work plastered with mud, and thatched with long rush-like grass; each consists of a single room, although in many a small part is screened off. The structure is supported by several rough wooden stanchions in the interior; and in the very centre of the floor is a small round concavity to serve as a fireplace, but as there is no outlet above, everything belonging to a Kafir smells strongly of smoke, which, however, is beneficial in one respect, as it effectually prevents the entrance of flies. The shape of the ordinary Kafir hut is a simple dome; that of a Fingo consists of a perpendicular circular wall surmounted by a dome-shaped roof, and often contains apertures to serve as windows; a kraal appearing at a distance like a circle of toadstools. The floors of many of these edifices are formed of a cement composed of clay and cowdung, called udaka, and in the Zulu country are often polished so brightly as to resemble black marble. The kraals are most frequently erected on a rising ground, and there are several footpaths leading down to a spot which invariably contains water; near them are plots of ground on which maize and millet are cultivated. A wealthy man is generally the owner of an entire kraal, some of which are of considerable size; each wife possesses a separate hut, others being used as storerooms. In the floor of the cattle enclosure several pits are excavated to serve as granaries; these are smoothly lined with udaka, and the mouth is covered with a flat stone and then earthed over: the maize, or mealies as this corn is termed in South Africa, when removed, is generally coated with mildew and possesses a disagreeable, cheesy smell, but this the Kafirs consider enhances the flavour. The seed mealies are stored in these pits still adherent to the cobs. The principal articles of diet are mealies, milk, pumpkins, and other gourds, and sweet potatoes; the mealies are beaten into meal between stones, and this, when boiled, forms an agreeable porridge, or they are parched in an iron pot. The milk they prefer in a sour state, as curds and whey, and it is made speedily to acquire this condition by exposure to the sun. Occasionally a man wishes to make a great show, and with this object he slaughters a bullock. All the neighbours seem to discover the fact by a kind of intuition: they require no invitation, but flock to the festive kraal, and soon nothing remains but the bones. The method of cooking flesh they generally adopt is to cut a large piece of meat into short strips leaving them connected by a small piece at the extremities, so that when complete it resembles somewhat a long string of sausages; this is thrown on the wood-ashes and imperfectly roasted. One end of a strip is then taken between the teeth and the other held in the fingers, while a mouthful is severed by an assegai with a kind of sawing motion. They also manufacture a kind of beer from the millet or Kafir corn; it is of a reddish hue, has considerable body, and in large quantities is an intoxicating liquor, generally leaving a racking headache.

Among the Xosa the dress of the men consists of a simple blanket of a dingy red colour, hanging from the shoulders; in their hands they invariably carry a long stick, with a small carved knob at the top, called induku. The women wear a well-fitting skirt of bullock's hide, with the red blanket gracefully drooping from the shoulders. One of the fore-arms is generally covered by a series of plain brass rings or coils of highly burnished brass wire; these are put on very tightly at first, and are often the cause of intense suffering, occasioning great inflammation of the hand, but all this is patiently borne for the sake of the ornamentation. On the opposite

The Kafir Tribes.

arm copper or steel bracelets are usually worn; while around the neck is a collar of teeth—those of a dog, or sheep, or jackal—but this collar is sometimes formed of scented wood. The belles often cover their faces, necks, and hands with red clay, leaving margins around the eyes and mouth, which they consider adds materially to their attractions, but which really gives them a weird, frightful appearance; they sometimes mix with this clay the juice of a strongly-scented plant, which has a broad, circular leaf, and grows in little knolls, and which they call safigani. When women pay a visit to a distant kraal, before reaching their destination they often sit down by a stream, and, wetting this clay, decorate themselves, the water serving as a mirror; some few, however, possess looking-glasses, which they have procured from the traders, when they never cease admiring themselves. They generally possess beautiful figures, although, as a rule, their faces are far from pretty. Both old and young are inveterate smokers, and they have a somewhat disgusting habit of constantly spitting. Their teeth are generally perfect and extremely white, forming a striking contrast with their sable skins; the constant mastication of mealies contributes towards this, and it is besides one of their occupations to sit by their fires of wood and rub their teeth with the ashes, and then wash them with water. The Fingoes, who have for many years lived under our protection, adopt occasionally the European costume, particularly if Christians; their women are especially grand on Sundays, affecting the most brilliant colours, quite regardless of the laws of contrast. The dress material is usually a gaudy print, such as one sometimes sees in the shop windows in England but never in the streets, so that one wonders what becomes of them. A tour among the fractionally Anglicized negroes of Africa would solve the enigma. The showy devices on what is known as trade cloth are moreover marvellous to behold. The vast majority of the Fingo females, however, still wear the red blanket, which is often made of a shaggy cotton material and ornamented profusely with rows of common shirt-buttons; they put on numerous bead ornaments, with a large beaded bag to serve as a pocket; whereas the bag of a Kafir woman is usually formed from the skin of a wild cat. Among the Zulus the only garment which the men wear is a kind of double apron behind and before, fastened round the waist by a string; it is composed generally of thin strips of dark hide, platted together, so as to form a series of long furry tails. The lobe of the ear is slit, and in the aperture is carried a long snuff-box, in shape like a common English needle-case. The snuff is composed of ground tobacco mixed with the ashes of the aloe plant: a small bone spoon is generally stuck in the hair. All the men who are married, or who have received the king's permission to marry, shave the top of the head, and wear around it a thick black ring termed Isikoko, formed of the folded hair coated with a resinous matter, which is then smoothed and polished. The skins of the more important chiefs often possess a fine gloss, the effect of some unguent; that of the king himself was especially cared for, the application being the fat of the lion; and it was usual, when one of these beasts was killed in the country, to send the fat to the sovereign. In his hand a Zulu carries three or four sticks, with a large carved knob at one extremity of each; these he uses as weapons, and can throw them with such dexterity as frequently to bring down a bird on the wing. A chief often provides himself with a finely carved, sharp pointed, ivory instrument, something like a paper-knife; with this he scrapes the perspiration from his skin, clears his nostrils, &c.; if less elegant, it is more cleanly than the pocket-handkerchief of civilization : many of them, likewise, wear a necklace of the claws of the lion or leopard, a small tuft of red eagles' feathers on the head, or the little wing feathers of a finch. The Zulu maiden or Intombi wears simply a small apron of beads fastened about the waist by a beaded band, usually of a pink colour. The married woman, or Umfazi, is dressed in a kilt, generally made of hide; she shaves the lower parts of the scalp, leaving a thick circular mat of hair on the summit of the head, which is dyed of a bright chocolate colour; and as they carry their burdens on the head it acts similarly to a porter's knot; they rarely smoke. The Zulus are a respectful and courteous people; when they pass one of their chiefs, or an English officer, they raise the right arm and point upwards with the fore-finger, at the same time exclaiming, "Inkosi," which means "Great Chief" or "Protector." The men of the Xosa tribes, like the women, are great smokers; their pipe has a very long bowl and short stem, and is generally made of metal;

their tobacco they cultivate themselves; their fire they usually procure from a flint and steel, which they buy of the traders, but sometimes by rubbing dry wood together; this is, however, a tedious and difficult process. A much more injurious habit to which they are addicted is the "Dakwa" smoking. The herb grows wild in damp kloofs, and resembles Indian hemp; it often produces a most intoxicating or maddening effect when smoked, and the process is somewhat curious. A bowl is fixed into the narrow end of a bullock's horn at right angles, the herb is placed in the bowl with a live ember, and the horn filled with water; the hand is then placed over the broad open end of the horn, and a mouthful of smoke drawn between the fingers and thumb; after two or three draws some water is conveyed to the mouth by means of an earthen cup; the end of a long hollow stick is then placed between the lips, through which is expelled both water and smoke; then a long whistle is given through the stick, and finally the smoker is seized with a long fit of coughing : and this process is repeated until the contents of the pipe are exhausted. Among the warlike Zulus, who mingle military ideas with every habit of daily life, a favourite pastime is for the Dakwa smokers to sit in a group, and, having made a smooth space on the ground, to expel beads of water through the hollow stick, with which they represent lines of warriors in different formations, and exercise their ingenuity in planning various methods of attack. I think it likely that the Kafirs have acquired this habit from the Arabs, and that it is a rude imitation of the Narguillah.

Polygamy obtains among the Kafirs. When a man wishes to marry, he has to purchase his wives, and he may possess as many as he can afford to buy: the ordinary price is from three to ten head of cattle, according to the lady's attractions. Of course this often leads to a great deal of bickering in after-life among the little community; one wife, when she desires to annoy another, taunting her as to the smallness of her value—"Ah, you only cost three head of cattle, while I was considered cheap at ten." The principal wife has her residence in a particular part of the kraal, and the remainder according to their rank. In Zululand, when the head of a kraal dies, the eldest son of his principal or favourite wife becomes the heir; and to him therefore belong all the other wives, even his own

The Kafir Tribes.

mother, his brothers, sisters, cattle, and everything else: if he is not of age, the eldest brother of the deceased takes the property in the meantime, and any children the brother may have by the widows belong to the son. Should there be no son, the brother is the heir. Similar laws obtain among most of the Kafirs. As soon as the cattle are paid, the wife is delivered over to her future husband; there is no recognized marriage ceremony, although a dance is often held. The wife takes with her, as a trousseau, a pot for cooking, a large stock of beads, a spare red blanket and skirt of bullock's hide, and a dancing equipment consisting of a long bag-like, richly-beaded cap, a leather belt thickly studded with brass buttons, and an ornament composed of numerous strings of beads to be worn round the chest. Should a chief know a wealthy man whom he considers a good match for his daughter, he sometimes sends her to him, and it is considered a great insult to refuse her, although the man has to pay handsomely in cattle; the daughter of an important chief often fetching from thirty to a hundred bullocks. Thus, if a man possesses several pretty daughters, they are a source of considerable wealth, and in special cases, even after marriage, the father continues to extort cattle year after year. It will be observed, as we proceed, that this as well as many of the Kafir customs are those of the other primitive pastoral races, of which records have been handed down to us. With them a girl is not, as a rule, permitted to choose her husband : if, after the bargain is concluded, she happens to detest him, she frequently runs away and returns to her father's kraal, or, if afraid to go there, she may seek refuge in some neighbouring hut. The husband starts in pursuit. In the former instance, before the father surrenders her, he generally stipulates for some additional cattle; but, wherever the husband discovers her, he invaribly administers a sound beating with his induku, or with a sjambok, before he conveys her back. Occasionally a solitary woman is met hurrying through the country with a large bundle on her head: this is almost certain to be a runaway wife: and she is often very cunning in her flight, for when she arrives at a drift she will cross it backwards, so that when her pursuer sees her footmarks in the mud, he may suppose it to be those of some one travelling in the opposite direction. Should a young Kafir re-

The Kafir Tribes.

quire a wife, and has not wherewith to buy one, his father may present him with a beast, and perhaps an uncle may give him another, and he then increases his stock by breeding; or he may possess three or four bullocks only, whereas the father of the girl may require ten for her. The latter will then often receive the three or four on account, simultaneously giving notice that, should the husband not pay the remainder by a certain time, the daughter will be taken back, and what he has already paid shall be forfeited. In this latter case the wooer too frequently sets himself to steal the number which is deficient, generally from some European settler, or from a colonist, as he knows that the latter cannot take the law into his own hands, or from some neighbouring tribe, or, failing this, from his own people: hence the native marriage laws are often indirectly one of the main causes of the wars in South Africa. The Kafirs are extremely skilful in tracing the spoor of their stolen cattle, following it for many miles, noting the direction in which every blade of grass is bent, and usually detecting the cattle in the very kraal to which they have been conveyed. Even then, however, it is not always that they recover them, for if they have been taken from a neighbouring people or tribe, directly that the thief brings them into his own territory his chief often claims half, and then, when the man is accused before that chief, the latter shields him, appearing quite ignorant of the whole transaction, and professing that the accuser is mistaken. They have also the most vivid recollection of their beasts : should a man lose one, and discover it a year or two afterwards, he would immediately recognize it and select it from among a large number. A remarkable feature in matrimony among some of the tribes is, that if the newly-married wife does not speedily acquire a paramour, the husband considers that she must be destitute of attractions, or that something else is wrong about her, and he either entirely neglects her, or perhaps dismisses her altogether. Among the Zulus marriage is made subservient to the military requirements.

Nearly all the manual labour in the country is performed by the women; in addition to tending the children and the domestic arrangements of the kraal, they cultivate the mealie patches entirely; they usually scatter the seed over the ground and hoe it in, except in cases where the husband owns a plough, when he will frequently condescend to use it. Between the mealie stalks they grow water-melons, vegetable marrows, and other gourds, sweet potatoes, and a dwarf scarlet-runner bean. These mealie patches are not fenced round, and a fresh piece of land is cultivated yearly, the old being allowed to lie waste. The Kafirs seem to be unacquainted with the use of manure. The boys of a family attend to the cattle, do the milking, &c.; while the man leads a thoroughly lazy life, roving about from kraal to kraal, prying into his neighbour's affairs, smoking, gossiping, and such-like. A Kafir is esteemed a boy until he arrives at about the age of eighteen, and during this period he is always dressed in a sheep-skin, and is fed on what his seniors leave. About this time he undergoes the process of circumcision, which rite at the present day is practised only by the Xosa tribes, and was probably acquired from the Mohammedan Arabs. Numbers of lads are generally circumcised at the same time. They are then divested of the sheepskin, and in its stead are provided with a kind of kilt formed of reeds or long grass; a similar thatch is placed round the neck, to spread over the upper part of the body; the head also is furnished with a covering of the same, shaped like a fool's cap: the bare parts of the body are then plastered over with white clay. Huts are provided for them at a distance from all other habitations, and no one has any communication whatever with them, unless it is to carry them food, but even then the bearer never approaches closely. Their period of exclusion, which generally occupies some weeks, is spent by them in dancing, which they generally do in the most frantic manner. This ceremony is termed "Amakweta," and the individuals are subsequently considered men, and are permitted to assume the red blanket, which is essentially the *toga virilis*. When a female arrives at puberty a dance is given, termed "Intonjani," to which all the young men and women of the locality receive invitations, and at which the most obscene orgies obtain: the girl in whose honour this is held is not herself present, but remains in a hut, concealed behind a mat. This dancing is sometimes kept up for several days. When a Kafir wishes to settle in a certain part of the country he applies to the chief of that district, who grants him permission to do so, and appoints him a spot on which to erect a kraal, with the right of pasturage for his cattle in the immediate vicinity, for there are no private estates, but all the land is in common. The location assigned by a chief is generally where there is most spare room, unless there is some man in his territory whom he desires to be rid of; then he may place the new comer very near him, with the object of annoyance.

Should a man be indicted for some crime before a great chief, who, as a rule, seems to possess a proper idea of justice and fair play, this chief will often sit for hours in the most stolid manner, and allow the disputants to continue expatiating on their differences without making a single remark, although he is paying the most rapt attention; at length perhaps one of them says something which contradicts an assertion he has made earlier in the day, when the chief is immediately down on him and concludes the case. The punishment is usually a fine of cattle; murder even is punished in this way, the cattle being mostly given to the murdered man's relatives. Should the criminal be unable to pay the cattle, his father or near relations have to do so; thus, should such a man be a systematic evil-doer, the property of the relatives is always in jeopardy. Such a one is generally quietly made away with by his friends, often through the agency of a witch doctor, or else notice is secretly conveyed to him of their intentions, so that he speedily makes off altogether.

It is extremely difficult to trace a man in Kafirland, for the kraals possess no distinctive names, and bear a close resemblance to each other, as do likewise the hills and kloofs; and it is only when one recognizes some well-known mountain or river that one is certain as to his whereabouts; even old traders have frequently to inquire the way. Should you ask a man where he lives, he will tell you, "At a certain river;" if you then require to know at what part of it, he will answer, "Close to such a mountain," which is perhaps as near as he can direct you.

When a Kafir dies, he is buried almost immediately, and should there be a convenient cave, or ant-bear hole, the body is doubled up and thrust in; otherwise, a grave three or four feet deep is dug, usually near the kraal. The corpse, enveloped in its blanket, is placed in the sitting posture, with the knees drawn up and the face turned towards the sunrise.

The Kafir Tribes.

The pipe and bag of the deceased are buried with him. The relatives shave their heads as a sign of mourning, and their friends do not visit them for several days afterwards, or until the principal relative pays the first visit; this is frequently done at a beer-drinking, which is an attraction that he cannot resist. Should a great chief die, several men, usually some of his councillors, are at once killed and buried with him.

The Kafirs are intensely superstitious. They all possess a firmly-rooted belief in witchcraft; and, indeed, this need not seem so very surprising when we think that so lately as the seventeenth century the King of England wrote a work on Demonology; that Matthew Hopkins received a public appointment as Witchfinder-General rather more than two centuries since; that as late as the year 1716 a child of tender years was hanged at Huntingdon for witchcraft; and in 1863 a poor, infirm old man died from the effects of a ducking he had undergone as a suspected wizard by some enlightened people of Essex. It has been calculated that for a period of 200 years in England alone, with a comparatively small population, an average of 150 people were yearly put to death at the hands of the law for this supposed crime. In Kafirland now, as in England then, this belief leads to incessant murder. Major Elliott, our intrepid Resident among the Tembus, informed me that, according to his estimate, 400 men perished annually from this cause among that tribe and their neighbours, the Pondos, Bomvanas, and Galekas. The determination on our part to prevent this was one of the causes which indirectly led to our war with the Zulus; and yet it must have been hard for that section of the English people who still rigidly adhere to the verbal inspiration of Scripture, to reconcile such a policy with the Mosaic text, "Thou shall not suffer a witch to live." A numerous and most influential class of men are the "witch" doctors so called; they are invariably consulted in every serious case of illness, which is almost always attributed to the malignity of a witch or wizard. They are also prominent in political matters, in which they are too frequently the tools of the more powerful chiefs. Such an impostor will, by his pretended dreams and prophecies, which he relates to the people, influence them exactly as the chief may wish. There are various kinds of doctors—war doctors, rain doctors, &c.—but, as a class, they are generally known to Europeans as witch doctors. A witch doctor, besides finding his profession very profitable, also enjoys certain privileges. Among other things he is exempted from military service. In the Zulu country, Ketchwayo, with his usual sagacity, saw the extent of the evil, and gave them an unmistakable hint that their numbers were not to be increased. Previous to a war, the warriors are all doctored, a bullock is taken, and a long incision made between his ribs with an assegai. The doctor then inserts his hand and lays open the aorta, so that the animal bleeds to death; it is then cut into small portions and sprinkled with medicine, after which a piece is given to all the warriors to make them courageous. A black mark is also painted on each man's forehead, and the doctor sells him a charm consisting of two or three small pieces of wood fastened to a string, so as to be tied round the neck; a morsel of this wood is masticated, and it is supposed to give them great courage, to render them invulnerable, and even to divert the course of a bullet. When a Zulu army is doctored, it forms a circle termed an Umkumbu; all the principal Indunas or chiefs, the doctors, and the king, if present, are in the centre; between them and the ordinary soldiers is a circle composed of the inferior chiefs; and the slaughtered beast having been cut into strips, these are taken round for each warrior to bite off a piece. Should a Kafir tribe become demoralized by defeat, and the witch doctor see that there is no hope of further gain, and that he may possibly incur the vengeance of some of the beaten clan, he usually contrives to slip away into the territory of some other tribe, assigning as a reason that he had discovered the presence of a doctor much more powerful than himself, against whose magical arts he was unable to stand. The prompting of some interested chief is often evident in their predictions; should these not be fulfilled the witch doctor is always ready with some excuse, which, however feeble and shallow, is readily believed; for instance, he will state that when he extracted his conclusions from the working of his charms, being in a great hurry at the time, he took the wrong kind of wood with which to make them, and so the mistake occurred. This explanation is satisfactory to the chief, and, of course, to the people. The witch doctors, or, as they might perhaps be termed with more propriety, the priests, become qualified for their professions in the following ways:—The office is very frequently hereditary, and apprenticeships are first served to an old witch doctor, who imparts his very small amount of knowledge; then, by voluntarily undergoing certain privations and self-imposed hardships, and by residing in solitude, so as to devote themselves to contemplation, and by listening to the sounds of the winds and the waves, they are supposed to obtain interviews with the Amahlosi, or spirits, who are considered always to inspire them. Having thus weakened both their physical and moral powers, they often fall into an ecstatic or dreamy condition, and on emerging from this the revelations they have received are presumed to constitute them accomplished practitioners. The Kafirs in almost every case attribute the cause of death, sickness—any extraordinary circumstance, in fact, such as a dog climbing over a hut—or any ill-fortune, to the midnight revels of witches and wizards, and the guilty person is termed an Umtakati. They have, indeed, a word Ukuzifela, which signifies "to die a natural death," but it is extremely rare to encounter a man who will employ that word when speaking of a departed relative. The Rev. Mr. Robertson, who has resided as a missionary among the Zulus for upwards of a quarter of a century, informed me: "Some years ago I kept a manuscript book entitled 'Death,' and of every man with whom I conversed I casually inquired whether his parents or other near relations were alive or dead, and, if the latter, how they had met their deaths. Nearly all, out of a vast number, had either been killed in battle, or by the king as Umtakatis." Their usual practice, more especially among the Zulus, is the following:— Whenever a man is sick, or should any ailment affect his wives or children or cattle, he at once goes to consult the Isanusi, or witch doctor, as to the cause and the remedy for it; but in ninety-nine cases out of a hundred he has probably made up his own mind as to its origin—that some person whom he dislikes, or who may have been his rival in love, has bewitched them; and he, accordingly, to translate literally the native idiom, "smells him out" as an Umtakati. The man respectfully approaches the Isanusi, sits down, and waits until he is addressed. He then hands his present to the sage; if a rich man, he might tender a bullock; if a poor person, a goat, a fowl, or an assegai. The doctor then accosts him, "You have some one ill?" The applicant beats the ground repeatedly with his stick. He then hazards a guess—"The patient is a man!" Should it be correct, the applicant again beats the ground rapidly; if wrong, he strikes it once. He then continues his guesses until he ascertains whether it is a man, woman, or child, and carries on his examination until he has wormed out all the details; he then proceeds to describe the case to the applicant, who has himself of course furnished all the information. He next decides whether the illness is occasioned by witchcraft, or whether it is a case for medicine. If the former, he proceeds to extract from the person whether there is any one he hates, or who has offended him, and will frequently determine that this is the person who is the cause of the mischief. Sometimes, to strengthen his case, the man will visit a second witch doctor, who, after subjecting him to a similar process of questioning, arrives at a similar decision. The man then reports the case to the principal chief of his district, who reports it to the king; then, if the accused is a wealthy man, and therefore worth plundering, an Impi, or armed party, is despatched to kill him. This Impi generally steals up during the night and lies in ambush, and as the accused emerges from his hut in the early morning he is either at once assegaied, or else captured, his shoulders violently dislocated, so as to disable him, and he is then either stoned or tortured to death by being impaled on a sharp stake. His wives and family are also often killed; any young daughters become the property of the king, as do also a certain proportion of the cattle, although he is rarely informed of the full number which the murdered man had; the remainder being divided between the owner of the bewitched person, the chief, and the Isanusi. The witch doctor sometimes informs his client that the spirits of his ancestors, for whom they have the greatest reverence, are angry with him for some reason or other, and to appease them he returns to his kraal and sacrifices a bullock; indeed, very few cattle are killed by the lower orders, unless under such circumstances. It is made a point of imperative importance that the services of an Isanusi should be secured whenever a person is sick, for, should the proprietor neglect to do so, his relations and friends would assail him, and very probably accuse him of being the Umtakati. Whenever a death occurs, they are careful to report it everywhere at once. Should the Isanusi decide that the case is one for medicine, he directs his client to go to a certain Inyanga. This man, who is distinct from the Isanusi in every respect, then visits the sick person; but before he proceeds to any examination a bullock has to be killed, upon which he is feasted. There is no doubt that these men do possess a few efficient drugs; for instance, they have discovered with us the use of the male fern root, and they have various powerfully stimulant and aromatic barks, but they endeavour to keep what little knowledge they do possess a profound secret. A certain Inyanga enjoyed a great reputation for being able to cure cattle of a kind of erysipelas, which attacks them in the spring. He was offered a large sum of money by a cattle owner if he would impart what his remedy was; but he declared that he would not do so for any amount. He was quite ready to treat the cattle, but not to do that. The Inyanga is generally experienced enough to see when a case is curable, or the contrary; if the former, he makes the most of it, and remains to eat and drink and administer his drugs; if the latter, he will probably give a dose of some medicine, and find an excuse for taking a speedy departure. Both the Isanusi and the Inyanga lay claim to inspiration from a source I have already described—"Ngipiwe," *i. e.* "I have been given," they will say. In most cases the Inyanga commences his treatment by purifying his patient, his hut, and indeed the whole kraal, by sprinkling medicated water everywhere; it is then necessary that a second bullock should be killed, for a two-fold purpose, viz. medicinally, and sacrificially to the spirits of the ancestors. Great cruelties are often practised upon the poor animal on such occasions. It is opened while alive, and the gall and other parts selected by the Inyanga cut out. The gall is always considered necessary, and it is sprinkled over the patient. The Inyanga then compounds an Imbiza, or pot, composed of a great number of medicines, in order that, if one fails, some other may be of use! I believe that these pots often hurry the poor patient out of the world. I know that in one case this occurred, for the Inyanga will often put herbs into these decoctions of the properties of which he is perfectly ignorant, and which may be highly poisonous; but a Kafir's faith in his medicine increases in proportion to its nauseousness. The Inyanga endeavours to act very strongly on the imagination of his patients: he appears before them with strings of medicines hanging round his neck, consisting of pieces of bark, roots, pieces of hide with the hair on, lumps of wax, pieces of bone, snakes, vertebræ, &c., and followed by a boy carrying more in a bag. If the case appears remedial, he declares with the utmost confidence that he knows all about it, and will be sure to effect a cure, no matter how many witches the patient may have against him. Among their remedial measures, one is to burn feathers and bunches of hair, and make the patient inhale the vapour; another is local bleeding. Should a patient suffer from a pain in a part, a number of short, shallow incisions are made, and a charcoal, produced by burning drugs in a crucible, rubbed in. Among the Amaxosa the witch doctor's methods are often somewhat coarser: should a person believe himself to be possessed by some evil influence, a favourite prescription is to direct the sufferer to place a live coal in his mouth for the purpose of driving it out; and when a man has some painful local affection, the doctor generally pretends that the sufferer is infested with some living thing in the part, a snake or beetle being the favourites. When sent for on such an occasion, he squats on his hams by the side of the sick person, surrounded by all the friends; and then he begins to explain the cause of the present illness, how many snakes there are inside the person, and all the people in the hut bow their heads very low, and say, "We agree." The following cases will further illustrate the system of the witch doctors :—A man, when out hunting, ran a thorn into his knee, which he at once extracted, but the part subsequently became inflamed. The doctor was sent for, and, after examining the part, told the man that there had been a beetle's egg at the end of the thorn, which had become hatched inside, and that the whole thing was due to the malice of a man who had bewitched him; "but," said he, "I'll soon find out the author of it." He then made a slight cut into the part, and sucked at it for some time; he then suddenly called out, "Ah! I've got him at last," and immediately spat out a good-sized beetle. He now told the patient to bathe it with a decoction of herbs, and give it rest, and it shortly got well. He then singled out a man against whom he doubtless had a spite, and declared that he had bewitched the other. This individual was arraigned before the chief, who fined him five head of cattle, part of which was awarded to the injured man, and part to the witch doctor for his skill. There was a Kafir living near Fort Bowker, in the Transkei, who remained loyal, and acted as a kind of upper servant to the officers of the F.A.M.P. (Frontier Armed and Mounted Police), the Galeka tribe having been driven across the Bashee. This man had a sick child of whom he was very fond, and he asked an English surgeon stationed there to see it, who said there was little use in prescribing, as the child must, from the nature of its disease, shortly die. This, however, did not satisfy the parent, who asked to be allowed to send across the river for a witch doctor. The sage came, looked at the child, and said that he must have a sovereign, and that the father must kill a couple of bullocks and make a feast that evening. This having been done, on the following morning he said that it was necessary to send for the assistance of another doctor. The officers of the F.A.M.P. here remonstrated with the father, and represented the folly and futility of the proceeding. But the man answered that from his childhood he had been taught to believe in their skill, and he persisted in sending for a second practitioner. This man arrived in due time, and said that he likewise must have a sovereign, and that a feast must be held similar to that on the preceding evening. The father told him that he had no bullock, but only two goats remaining; he was then directed to kill them, and the banquet was given. The doctors afterwards held a consultation, and, as the result, informed the man that some enemy of his had deposited a very powerful poison under the floor of the hut, which was killing the child; but as soon as it was sufficiently light in the morning they would unearth it, at the same time ordering out all the guests in case that they also should suffer. They then left themselves, but almost immediately discovered the hut to be on fire, and raised a tremendous alarm, so that the child was got out. They afterwards explained that the poison was so terribly powerful that it had actually ignited the hut, and that it was fortunate they had been sent for to detect it, or the child might have been burned to death. Early the next morning they recrossed the Bashee, having got all they could, and death shortly removed the child.

Should a chief wish to destroy a man, either on account of some pique or because he covets his possessions, he takes advantage of any illness in his family to summon the witch doctor, who receives directions to "smell out" the culprit. The doctor goes to work and soon says that he has discovered the man, who perhaps lives near such a river; the chief returns that the man from whose sorceries his family is suffering does not live that way at all, but in a certain direction, which he points out—at last perhaps naming the very man, in which opinion the doctor coincides. After this the usual scene of bloodshed occurs. One of our residents among the Kafirs informed me that a short time since he met with such a case. A boy came running to his residency to say that they were murdering his mother at a kraal some two miles distant. He immediately started on horseback and found that the entire kraal had been burned and everything carried off, the unfortunate owner having been "smelt out" as a wizard. He succeeded in tracing the spoor to the bank of a neighbouring river, where he found the body of the man with the abdomen ripped up, and the corpse pierced by so many assegai wounds that they could not be counted; he also found assegais sticking in the ground, which had evidently been thrown at the man as he was running. He further traced the spoor to the kraal of a neighbouring chief, whom he seized and carried to his residency, together with a witch doctor who was on the spot. He then tried the case, and, finding them guilty, had the chief given fifty lashes; but the witch doctor unfortunately escaped, and had not since been seen in the district. The chief went with his back all bleeding to the nearest mission station and complained. The missionary, with that most dangerous infatuation for which certain people in England are notorious whenever a negro appears on the scene, became very irate, and deeply sympathized with him, exclaiming at the heinousness of flogging a man of his standing and influence—little being thought of the fearful murder which he had committed, or of the deceased man's family, which was reduced from affluence to beggary.

Should a chief die, unless from sheer old

The Kafir Tribes.

age, nothing will convince his tribe that he died a natural death, and the witch doctor soon "smells out" the man who has been the cause, and who suffers death in consequence; and such is the deeply-rooted belief in the doctor's sagacity and skill, that the victim himself will not deny it, but thinks that the doctor must know better than he, and that he must have contributed to the chief's death unconsciously.

In seasons of drought they apply to a rain doctor to procure a fall of rain. He sometimes holds a dance at his hut, or lies outside and goes through several manœuvres with sticks, sending men into the kloofs to procure a particular wood, and doing other things which are believed to have the desired effect.

The system of espionage practised among Kafirs is remarkable. A Zulu chief some time since visited a missionary for the purpose of procuring some strychnia to poison panthers: having received it, he inquired how much would be necessary to poison a man, and was greatly amazed at the smallness of the quantity. He then said that he would not for the world take the poison to his kraal, for his life would not be safe; he could not poison the trap without some single person

at any rate seeing him, and he could not trust
that person. He remarked that he could only
really rely on a white man; but he did not
ascribe this to any virtue existing among the
white race, but it was an inherent habit
which they could not resist.

Some of their ideas are very curious.
Baboons, which are very common in South
Africa, they regard with intensely superstitious feelings; they believe that they never
die or reach mature old age, but that they
are capable of rejuvenescence. A wizard
often rides on a baboon at night, from kraal
to kraal, to deposit some noxious herb where
the person resides whom he wishes to injure.

Lightning they regard as a bird; the zig-
zag flash they believe to be the legs, and the
thunder its voice; they call it Upundulu.
They are much afraid of a thunderstorm, and
often summon a witch doctor to protect
them: this individual will stand at the door
of a hut with a stick, and, when there is an
unusually vivid flash, he will make a blow at
it, saying, perhaps, "There! you see that the
Upundulu was nearly in here then, but I was
too much for him and kept him out;" then
probably afterwards a more distant and less
brilliant fork appears, when the doctor

immediately takes credit to himself, "There! you observe how afraid he is of me, and has kept further away this time." Frequently, of course, one of these impostors cannot be procured, when the owner of the hut will stand during the storm inside his door with a handful of assegais, and each time the lightning flashes he drives his assegai across the aperture into the ground to try and kill the bird, which he believes is endeavouring to effect an entrance. Should a hut be stricken, they attribute it to the ferocity of the Upundulu, which has entered in spite of all their precautions, and the inhabitants of the entire kraal will desert their homes until the witch doctor, by his arts, has purified the place.

A Kafir, as a rule, possesses a great antipathy to going to sea; and, indeed, it is not a matter for wonder that they have no maritime proclivities, seeing that there are neither creeks nor harbours along the entire coast, but that everywhere a perpetual surf rolls. They imagine that immediately they crossed the horizon they would fall down on the other side.

They consider that the sun of a morning comes out of a large hole, passes over them, and then returns behind the sea to his hole, from which he again emerges the following morning. Their notions as to the cause of a rainbow are singular: they imagine that a gigantic snake exists, which, however, only a very few of their greatest doctors have ever seen, and they regard the rainbow as a reflection of this snake's eye.

In journeying about the Transkei, one occasionally encounters a pile of small stones near the footpaths, which have their origin in the following custom:—Should a Kafir be going in search of a wife who has decamped, or in quest of some girl he wishes to marry, or should he have stolen some cattle and is being chased by the owners, or should he be engaged in any similar pursuit, he throws a stone on the heap, saying, as he does so, "May I have luck!" The auspicious spots where these piles have accumulated have been primarily discovered and marked by the witch doctors.

The old women, especially among the Zulus, are fond of frightening the children and young girls with marvellous stories. They are generally about wizards or witches, or the Amanzima or men-eaters; they represent the latter as huge heavy beings like men, who prowl at night or during thick misty weather; behind their shoulders they are furnished with a large fleshy basket, in which they place any children they may catch; they then walk away to a rock or precipice, which opens and lets them into a cave, where they cook and eat the children. And in this way they so terrify the young people that they are greatly afraid to go outside the hut at night, or during a fog. A favourite story is of a party of travellers, who, becoming very tired and hungry, entered a large ant-bear hole, which extended for a long distance underground and terminated in a large cave: here, sitting down, they untied their bundles and began to cook and eat their food. While thus engaged, a 'Nzima comes to the entrance of the cave with a lot of pumpkins which he has collected: his forefinger is furnished with a nail as large as a great shovel; with this he slices up his pumpkins, all the while observing the people in the cave, but pretending that he does not. Soon there enters a second 'Nzima, and they consult together, giving hungry glances at the travellers, the terror of whom is vividly narrated; but these at last manage to outwit the Amanzima and make their escape.

Their conception of a God is very hazy: they have some idea of a kind of First Cause, or Creator, but do not appear to have any name for God in their language; the word Tixo is, however, used by some of them, but this they have borrowed probably from the Hottentots, as they have Satanos, or Devil, from the missionaries. A Kafir regards himself as the only being worthy of veneration, and next to himself his cattle. When he is sworn in a resident magistrate's court, he is directed to raise his arm and hold up his fore and middle fingers; then some such dialogue as the following ensues:—

Q. "Do you believe anything?"
A. "I don't know what you mean."
Q. "Do you believe in cattle?"
A. "Yes."
Q. "Do you believe in women?"
A. "Yes."
Q. "Do you believe in yourself?"
A. "Well, yes."
Q. "Do you believe there is a God?"
A. "Well, the missionaries say there is, but we've never seen Him."

They believe in existence after death, and that they are destined to go below the earth, where they will rejoin their ancestors and departed cattle. I have mentioned before the veneration they possess for the spirits of their ancestors; this must exist most strongly when they are so self-denying as to sacrifice cattle to them. On such an occasion, and more particularly in the Zulu country, a man assembles all his friends around the cattle kraal; he then delivers an address, in which he expatiates on the glories of his forefathers, especially with reference to their military achievements, enumerating them even some six or seven generations back. He then slaughters a bullock and makes a feast, a piece of the flesh being placed at the back of the hut for the spirits; this, perhaps, will be thrown away on the following day, but still they think that the spirits are satisfied. These spirits are known in the Kafir language as Amahlosi, and everything that happens, whether good or bad, proceeds from them. In the latter instance it is considered necessary to propitiate them by sacrifice; in the former they are panegyrized before the sacrifice, as above described. Some persons would regard this as an instance of the lamentable darkness overshadowing these people; but is it more extraordinary than are some of the doings of the Spiritualists in the midst of civilized communities?

Kafirland abounds in venomous serpents, and the natives generally kill them unless they enter their huts; then they believe that they are animated by an ancestral spirit, and leave them unmolested. As the snake enters all the inmates depart, and do not return until it has left. A missionary informed me that he was conducting a service in his little church when he detected the peculiar hissing of a snake under the Communion table; having concluded the prayers prematurely, he cautiously looked beneath, and discovered a black "Mamba," perhaps the most venomous of South African serpents. He directed some of the congregation to kill it, when they informed him that they had seen it for some time, but would not disturb it, as they thought it might be a relation of his. There are special snakes, of a yellowish colour, which they always regard as animated by an ancestor, and they term them Amahlosi; these they will never molest under any circumstances. Here we have instances of the ancient doctrine of Metempsychosis. They consider that the Creator formed all things out of a bed of reeds, and they account for

The Kafir Tribes.

death by saying that, when man was first made, the Creator sent a chameleon to give him life, and afterwards a lizard to convey death; but the lizard being the quicker reptile arrived first, and so death arose.

When the Amaxosa are at war, a considerable proportion of the men, perhaps a third, carry some fire-arm, of which one sees the most extraordinary variety, from the old flint-lock brass-mounted musket to the present Snider rifle, and every one carries a bundle of assegais, the blades of which are encased in a kind of quiver of bullock's hide. These blades are of different shapes, and each weapon possesses a distinct name; there are six at least, called 'Gnola, 'Gnana, 'Gnanda, Izaka, Iskilta, and Isigexla; they manufacture them from old horse-shoes, files, or any old metal, and they keep them very sharp by rubbing them against stones. The Zulus smelt their own iron, which exists in large quantities in their country, and their assegais are made much better and are more highly finished than those of the Xosa. An assegai is known among the Kafirs as Umkonto; in addition to being used as a weapon of war, it is made to serve much the same purposes as an English clasp-knife. The assegais of the Xosa are used principally as missiles; there are a few, however, specially made for stabbing at close quarters, or for despatching a wounded enemy. When an army sustains a defeat, it immediately breaks up into small bodies of from three to ten, who "trek" about the country in search of food, and collect again at some place appointed by the general. This renders the country particularly unsafe, for it is impossible to enter any kloof, or other place where there is the least cover, without the greatest chance of encountering some of them. When at war, a Kafir possesses but one idea, and that is the destruction of his foeman; such an attribute as mercy is beyond his comprehension; he cannot understand kindness from an enemy. He knows that Englishmen give quarter, but he does not attribute this to any moral goodness on their part, but rather regards it as an inherent impulse in their nature which they are unable to resist; similarly the prosecution of vengeance is with him irresistible. They never spare a wounded foe, but stab him to death with an assegai, working the blade round in the body, simultaneously making a horrible yelling noise. They usually lay open the abdomen to prevent the corpse swell-

The Kafir Tribes.

ing from decomposition, for they have a superstition that, were the dead body to swell, they would do so likewise. The fallen man perhaps sees his victorious enemy advancing towards him, and is perfectly aware of his object; he looks on what is about to happen as quite a matter of course; he makes no appeal for mercy, and receives his death wound without a murmur. When planning an attack they always consider the means of retreat in case of a reverse, and a favourite time for carrying their plans into execution is in the early morning, or during the latter part of the afternoon—probably in this case that, if worsted, they may retreat under cover of the darkness. It is usual in war-time to see the sky-lines of the hills dotted with men on the look-out: should they descry a small party of white men, they will rapidly creep in considerable numbers to some appointed spot, and lie concealed in the long Tambooki grass, with which the country abounds, until the white men pass, and then they take them by surprise: in such cases they never attack unless they greatly outnumber the whites. The Kafirs are warlike from their earliest years; even the young children practise throwing the assegai, by rolling a large bulb along the ground, and hurling sharply-pointed sticks at it when in motion; this is a favourite pastime with the boys when tending the cattle. Although the Kafir shows himself such a complete savage during war, in times of peace he is not without his good qualities; he possesses gratitude, generosity, and honesty, except where cattle are concerned. The Fingo, on the contrary, is a cool, calculating, business-like man, who always takes time to consider what he can make out of you.

The Kafirs, like many other black races, strongly resemble children; they have a very keen sense of the ridiculous, and exhibit a great deal of good temper. Should you chase one, or imitate his voice, or make a grimace, he will laugh most heartily. They possess wit also. When the Kafir war commenced, the principal witch doctor gave the Galekas a charmed word, "Wabasha," which they were to shout whenever they fired at an enemy, and then the bullet would be sure not to miss. As the Galekas got worsted, and our Fingo allies began to gain the upper hand, they used it, on meeting the enemy, as a term of ridicule. When small parties approached, preparatory to a skirmish, they would sometimes enter into a discussion about the war, as they have

The Kafir Tribes.

most powerful voices and converse at great distances, until at last, perhaps, some Fingo would shout "Wabasha," which usually angered their opponents very much, and brought matters to a crisis.

These people often show much respect for old age; they do not like killing old men, and often regard an old man's words with a species of veneration. When on a hill-side, sitting on my horse near Veldtman, the head man of the Fingoes, watching the progress of a skirmish just below, an old man approached him and delivered a long discourse, to which Veldtman listened most attentively, and subsequently had it repeated by evidently a special orator to a large number of his troops. After his departure I inquired of Veldtman as to who he was, but he answered that he "did not know, probably one of Smith Poswa's people" (the name of another Fingo chief). I then applied to the latter, supposing that he was some man of note, but he replied, "No, quite a common old man." I noticed near me also a young Fingo warrior, with a white goat's beard attached to his chin, and I requested him to inform me why he wore it. "Ah," he answered with a grin, "when we fight Galekas dey take me for ole man—ha! ha! ha!"

The Kafirs are often very figurative in their ideas: when they form a cordon round a place, so as to prevent any egress of the enemy, the warriors scatter so as to cover a large space; this they term "sowing themselves," in allusion to the way in which the mealies are disseminated when planted. Some peaceably disposed Galekas once sent two bullocks to a company of our troops stationed near; one possessed a perfectly white body with a black head, to denote that it was a present from the black to the white man; the other was a red bullock with a white head, to indicate that it was sent to the white-faced men who wore red coats. The Zulus are adepts at discerning a man's special attributes, and they usually know him among themselves by a metaphorical term denoting this; thus, Mr. John Dunn's Zulu name signifies "The hawk that strikes but does not eat;" another European is known as "The man who blusters," and so on.

The transport in war-time is carried on by the huge waggons of the European settlers, drawn by a team of from twelve to sixteen bullocks known as a "span;" they are driven

The Kafir Tribes.

by natives armed with immensely long whips, while a boy, termed a "Vorluper," leads the two foremost oxen by means of a noose of hide called a "reim." Each bullock has his especial name, which he seems to know perfectly; they all appear to end in *man* or *maun*—the most common are "Vorkmaun," "Shonteelmaun," probably the Kafir pronunciation of gentleman; "blessmaun," which is applied to an animal with a good deal of white on his forehead, and "Inglemaun," corruption of "Englishman," which latter animal is popularly said to receive more flogging than any other in the span. When they ascend a hill, or come to a difficult part of the road, the yells and screams of the drivers and the cracking of whips are almost deafening. A heavily-laden-waggon often gets stuck fast in a "drift," and then spans of oxen are unyoked from the accompanying waggons and attached so as to form one very long span, with which the waggon, if a sound one, is at length extricated; should this accident occur to one of the foremost waggons, the march of a column of troops is seriously delayed. When they wish to stop a span, the vorluper guides the heads of the two leading bullocks to one side of the road, simultaneously throwing clods at the hinder ones, which has the desired effect. These "trek oxen" are well trained to their duties. When the time for in-spanning arrives, the drivers go out and give a call with which the animals are familiar; then they may be seen coming in all directions from the grazing grounds towards the camp. Each span is driven to its own waggon, where the cattle stand in straight lines to be haltered with reims, after which they form two deep, to be attached to the yokes.

The natives of Kaffraria know our soldiers as the "Amajohnny," "Johnny" being the term by which a soldier usually addresses a Kafir; they are popularly supposed to enter the world attired in a red coat, and a small drummer is regarded as one of the Amajohnny in the stage of infancy. Previous to the landing of the Naval Brigade of H.M.S. "Active," no blue-jackets had been seen in their country, so they were somewhat puzzled what to call them. Eventually they knew them as "Blessmaun," after the cattle before mentioned, our men all wearing white covers to their caps.

A considerable exportation of wool and hides takes place from the Transkei, especially

The Kafir Tribes.

from those parts set aside as Government reserves. When encamped near the main drift of the Great Kei River, I was kept awake nearly the whole night by the incessant rattle of the heavily-laden waggons crossing into the colony, so that the trade must be very extensive. Of course the great drawback to the commercial development of the Transkei is the want of a proper harbour, there being no place along the coast which would afford shelter to a single vessel, but everywhere a mighty surf thunders on the shores. The nearest approach to a harbour is that at East London; but here a formidable bar exists at the mouth of the Buffalo River, the crossing of which, excepting in very fine weather, is attended with much risk.

THE KAFIR COUNTRY.

REMARKS ON THE TRANSKEI AND ZULULAND.

THAT which first strikes the stranger on his arrival in the Galekaland, or Transkei, is its smallness, from the River Kei to the Bashee, as the crow flies, being only some fifty miles, and its widest measurement, from the Fingo country to the sea, is about thirty miles. It consists of long chains of hills or grassy downs, the bases of which meet in such a way as to impart to the valleys a dove-tailed aspect. Some of these hills form lofty elevations deserving the name of mountains, the principal of which are the 'Mbongo near the Bashee, Quintana or Centani towards the Kei, Gandana in the North, and Incanga almost central. Along the tops of these downs are the only roads, consisting merely of waggon tracks formed by the traders who visit the country. This renders travelling pleasant, as one always commands an extensive view. Besides the two large rivers already mentioned, there are several second-rate ones, viz. proceeding eastward from the Kei, the Xoxo, Kologha, Robinaba, Cogha or Quora, Jujuga, Shexweni, Xnabaxana, and Xnabasa; but almost every kloof contains its stream, so that it is in reality a well-watered country; the water being, moreover, of considerable purity, excepting towards the sea coast, where it is frequently brackish. The soil is in general good, extending to a considerable depth; it is usually of a deep black hue, but in some districts chocolate or Indian red, the underlying strata consisting of reddish non-fossiliferous sandstone. It bears the plough well, and under the care of an English agriculturist could not probably be excelled in point of productiveness; its verdure is magnificent, and, indeed, I should consider it the garden of South Africa. The kloofs are in general well wooded, many of them containing very fine timber, the numerous shades of green in the foliage having a most pleasing effect. A rivulet, clear as crystal, usually meanders over beds of slab-like sandstone, the huge gnarled roots of the trees crossing in many places dam the water, forming large natural basins, from which the current proceeds onwards by means of pretty cascades, the banks being richly fringed with delicate maiden-hair ferns; numerous woody creepers ascend, forming spiral coils around the trunks of the trees, or hanging in graceful festoons or rope-like from the branches; the green carpet, consisting in great part of many beautiful varieties of ferns, gaudy with intervening flowers, and flecked with patches of sunlight, in which the most brilliantly feathered butterflies sport; above green parrots wing their way, while generally a sublime silence reigns. Moore contemplated some such scene when he wrote,

> "I'll seek by day some glade unknown,
> All light and silence like Thy throne."

The climate is delightful during the greater part of the year; the heat is sometimes oppressive in the summer, rarely, however, exceeding 82°; it is in general tempered by a cool, refreshing, south-easterly breeze, which springs up early in the afternoon. A good deal of rain falls annually, the winter being the drier season; in the autumn, thunderstorms are frequent. It is altogether a most healthy country, and proper sites for residences being selected, I do not think there could possibly be a better resort for persons suffering from certain pulmonary diseases.

Galekaland would be a paradise to a naturalist; both its *fauna* and *flora* are numerous and varied. Among those commonly encountered on a march are several kinds of buck, and occasionally an eland, baboons, and wild cats. A wonderful variety of insects is found in the Veldt, especially of the locust tribe—one in particular, met with everywhere, possessing bright yellow wings, and is usually at first mistaken for a butterfly; troublesome ticks in myriads, which trespass on both man and beast; *mantis religiosa*, and other kinds; magnificent butterflies and huge variegated moths. Among the birds, snipe, grey plover, quail, bustards, and partridges. Game in general would be plentiful if not so perseveringly hunted by the natives, for nothing is either too small or too young for a Kafir to kill. Large and small locust birds—the former a tall, very fine creature, with long legs like a heron; green parrots, cranes, pigeons, sugar-birds (*nectarinia*), hawks, carrion crows, ass-vogels, and turkey buzzards; serpents, from the terrible puff adder down to the beautiful little grass snakes; iguanas, frogs, lizards, fluvial crabs, small scorpions, and centipedes. Although snakes are without doubt plentiful, they are not frequently met with; among them is a small whip snake of a most irascible nature—when trodden on or attacked, it will, if possible, coil round any part of the aggressor and administer a series of bites in rapid succession. There is also the python, which grows to a length of from eight to twenty feet, and is in some cases as thick as a man's thigh. Should a native kill one of these serpents, and it becomes known, his life is never afterwards safe, as there is a widespread superstition that, if a man can drink the gall of a person who has slain a python, it renders him very courageous; consequently he is always being dogged by some chief intent on obtaining his liver. So if the Kafirs should kill in battle a very brave enemy, one whom they have remarked as conspicuous for his courage, they remove his heart, and a small piece is eaten by each warrior with a similar idea.

Among the *flora* may be mentioned the many *genera* of beautiful ferns, including the tree fern; they grow in every place where there is the least shade and moisture; in the kloofs, of course, they are most abundant, but every ant-bear hole usually contains a fine bunch of fronds. These holes are formed by the ant-bear, which burrows beneath the ant-hills, so as to sweep the interior with his long tongue; the upper part, being thus undermined, soon falls down under the influence of rain, and a small cave remains. There are various *labiatæ*, many highly scented; fungi, the edible *Agaricus campestris* being especially abundant after rains; everlastings, a small, many-flowered variety, forming a kind of corymb, grow everywhere amid the waving grass; several variously coloured *gladioli*, nine in number at least; *convolvuli*, with blue, white, and scarlet *corollæ;* a prickly solanaceous plant, bearing a yellow globular fruit, and forming an impenetrable fence around the kraals; the Cape gooseberry (*Physalis pubescens*), also one of the *solanaceæ;* a dwarf briar, bearing very fine blackberries; tobacco in the neighbourhood of kraals; and a liliaceous plant resembling the squill, the dried layers of the bulb of which is a good application for sealing up recent wounds; and every Kafir, when at war, carries a piece in his bag. A prickly mimosa tree, bearing fragrant yellow flowers, flourishes in every part of South Africa. There are two large forests in the Transkei, the Udwessa and the Manubi.

The Kafir Country.

The climate of Zululand is almost tropical, and much of the vegetation found in tropical regions flourishes, especially in the low-lying districts towards the sea coast; here several kinds of palm-trees are found fringing the low sandy ridges, or growing in clumps. These lowlands consist of a vast undulating plain, traversed by rivers, which become so swollen during the summer or rainy season, especially after the heavy thunderstorms, which are frequent, that many parts of the district become converted into marshes. The reason why these rivers so commonly overflow is that their mouths are traversed by bars, and, unless the volume of water during the rainy season is sufficient to force a passage through them, a rise must occur. The mouths of the larger rivers are expanded into permanent lagoons: there is a considerable one at the mouth of the Umslatoosi, while that at the mouth of the Umvalosi is so extensive as to be known as St. Lucia Bay. These rivers, proceeding in a north-easterly direction along the coast from the Tugela (Zulu, Utukela), are—the Inyoni, Umsundusi, Amatakulu, Inyezane, Umlalazi, Umslatoosi, and Umvalosi. These coast districts are, during the summer and autumn,

November to May, very unhealthy, dysentery and remittent fever being common. The temperature is high in summer, averaging from 82° to 92° in the shade; in the winter also the days are warm, but there is an unusual disproportion between the day and night temperatures. From the records I kept I find that during the month of June, about midwinter, while the former gave an average of 82°, the latter was 48°, the maximum by day during this period was 95° the minimum by night 43°. With regard to geological formation, Zululand consists almost entirely of yellow sandstone; granite is found in the most elevated parts; the soil along the coast is remarkably red, containing a considerable quantity of iron; limestone is rarely met with; there is a fine clay, beautifully plastic; and coal is found in many parts. A waggon conductor, who accompanied our column, and who was an ex-miner, found a seam which he ascertained to be some seven feet thick and of excellent quality, and with which he made a fire, very much to the astonishment of some Zulus, who had regarded it merely as black stone. The country is generally said to consist of three terraces, rising one above the other, the lowest being the coast

The Kafir Country.

country; the interior comprises some very high lands, one mountain exceeding six thousand feet: many of the highest parts are covered with wood, and in the winter severe frosts are common. The north-east wind is fresh and dry, but in the coast districts is considered unhealthy, on account of being impregnated with malaria from the extensive swamps about St. Lucia Bay. The south-west is the rainy wind; it prevails during the summer: towards the middle of April comes the latter rain, called among the Zulus by a name signifying "The rotter of the mealie stalks." The average rainfall for a year is about thirty-four inches. The country during the autumn is everywhere covered with very high grass, often attaining six or seven feet; this is fired in all directions by the natives, in order that young grass may afterwards spring up to support the cattle during winter. Some extensive forests exist; and among the lowland vegetation are commonly found several kinds of palm, as before mentioned, and especially that known as "the traveller's palm," pines, *hibisci*, leguminous shrubs, *aurantiaceæ liliaceæ*, mimosa, orchids, *euphorbia*, Cape gooseberry, and the *amatungulu* plum. Among the wild animals are rarely elephants and lions, leopards, jackals, hyænas, buffaloes, hippopotami, buck, and quaggas: these have been diminishing in numbers yearly since the introduction of fire-arms, and with them is gradually disappearing the tetsi fly, the bite of which was not unfrequently fatal, even to a horse. Some forty kinds of serpents exist, all, with but few exceptions, being venomous; the most dreaded are the puff adder, which is very common, and the black mamba, sometimes attaining a length of ten feet, which, under certain circumstances, becomes very aggressive; the python attains a length sometimes of fifteen or twenty feet. Alligators are found in most of the rivers. One of the greatest pests to travellers in the lowlands is the lung sickness; it affects those animals principally which are allowed to graze in low, damp situations, especially when the dew is on the grass, and sometimes decimates the horses.

THE KAFIR WAR.

CAMPAIGN OF THE NAVAL BRIGADE AGAINST THE KAFIRS, 1877—78.

In a leading article of one of our principal English newspapers, towards the end of November, 1877, was to be seen the following:— " We are likely soon to have another Kafir war on our hands." The term " Kafir War" has become a familiar one in England, as indeed it well might, since there were affairs of this kind in the years 1819, 1835, 1846, and in 1850, which is known as the " Great Kafir War ; "again, in 1856, the Kafirs were for some time on the very verge of an outbreak, and were only prevented, partly by the energetic action of General Jackson, and partly by the scarcity of food. Kreli, with the idea that he would compel every Kafir to fight with desperation, having prevailed on a witch doctor, Umhlakazi, to predict that, should they destroy all their crops and cattle, their forefathers, with their departed cattle, would rise from the earth and drive the white race into the sea, which prophecy was generally acted on. These wars have often been of a most unsatisfactory nature, the Kafirs taking to the bush, from which they maintained a prolonged guerilla warfare, attacking convoys and slaughtering parties of men whenever a chance presented; and the attempt to dislodge them has often led to a lamentable loss of life. In the present campaign the enemy showed himself more in the open than formerly; this was probably owing to the confidence engendered by the more general possession of fire-arms. The tribes engaged were the Gaikas, who owned Sandilli as their paramount chief, and occupied the eastern parts of the Cape Colony, termed British Kaffraria, or the Ciskei; and the Galekas, who inhabited the country between the Kei and Bashee Rivers, known as the Transkei. Kreli, son of Hintza, was paramount chief of the latter. Included among the Gaikas is the T'slambi tribe, so named after a chief of that name who flourished towards the end of the last century, and who assisted the Dutch colonists against the natives. Their chief, some

The Kafir War.

years since, was Umhala, several of whose sons still reside in the country, as Dimba and Smith Umhala. The prefix "Smith" is sometimes met with among these people, who occasionally take other European names; this is adapted from Sir Harry Smith, formerly governor of the colony.

The northern parts of the Transkei, as well as districts in British Kaffraria, have been for many years occupied by the Fingoes (Amafengu), at present a powerful and numerous tribe, formerly slaves of the Galekas; but, having revolted and allied themselves with us during our war with that tribe under Hintza, in 1835, they were placed in their present position by the British Government. This people had long been an eyesore to the Galekas, who viewed with bitter feelings their old slaves flourishing as an independent tribe, in possession of a large portion of what was formerly their country; and it is not surprising that they should have been desirous of driving out not only the Fingoes, but also their white supporters with them. Having this object in view, these sections of the Amaxosa had for a long time previously been covertly increasing their stocks of firearms, and most of their weapons, painful to relate, were supplied by certain colonists known as "gun runners:" traders' waggons were occasionally encountered in the Transkei containing arms and ammunition cleverly concealed. Near Butterworth, a populous place in Fingoland, but on the Galeka frontier, the authorities were in one instance about to interfere; but the proprietor of the waggon, having by some means received timely information, crossed the small stream and entered the Galeka country, where he could not be touched. The first moon of the new year was the time commonly reported to have been fixed for a general rising, the new moons being regarded as auspicious seasons; but, as far as the major part of the Kafirs was concerned, the outbreak was premature; the chiefs rose in succession instead of doing so simultaneously, and to this fact, coupled with the destructive power of the breech-loading rifle, a weapon which the natives fearfully underrated, and perhaps to the incapacity of the present generation of chiefs, must be attributed the salvation of a great part of the Eastern Colony. The first hostile collision occurred at a Fingo "beer-drinking" near Butterworth. Many people conversant with the habits of the Galekas are of opinion that Kreli purposely arranged this, and so precipitated matters; others consider that the *émeute* was accidental. Whatever may have been the origin of the affair, several Galekas appeared on the scene, a son of Mapassa, one of Kreli's most powerful chiefs, being amongst them. They behaved in the most insolent manner, high words ensued, followed by a fight, in which some men were shot: among the latter were two Galekas notorious as being amongst the most turbulent of the tribe, and it is not improbable that these men were specially selected for the occasion, so as to ensure a quarrel and thus begin the war. There is little doubt that, had not this war commenced when it did, it would unquestionably have occurred in the course of a year or two. The Galekas had not only been for a long period gradually accumulating fire-arms, but Kreli had been inviting every one of the tribe he could find to come and settle in his territory, until it had become greatly over-populated. Segaio, the son of Kreli, appears to have possessed even more influence than his father among the younger men of the tribe, and they did not doubt that success was certain, possessed as they were of such a multitude of fire-arms. These longed for action, but, after his experience of former wars, Kreli himself was cautious; he asserted that the quarrel was only with the Fingoes, and not with the white man. He had the missionaries safely conducted across his frontier, partly, doubtless, from magnanimous motives engendered by personal friendship, but partly also as a "blind." He knew most certainly that the English would not permit the Fingoes to be crushed, but it was a cunning policy on his part to endeavour by temporizing to delay any assistance as long as possible. The wily Mapassa quickly comprehended the aspect affairs were likely to take, and surrendered to our Government. His Excellency Sir Bartle Frere, Governor of the Colony, anxious to adjust matters, summoned Kreli to meet him: the chief refused, and then the Governor, who so perfectly grasps the situation, and understands how to exercise that ready firmness which is the only true method of dealing with savage races, deposed him from his chieftainship, and confiscated his country as far as the Quora River. Kreli, or Se-kreli as his people term him—that being the native pronunciation of Zachariah, the Christian name of a Dutchman after whom he was called—although a firm patriot, is described by those who know him intimately as a man of a generous temperament, complaisant to Europeans, and an impartial administrator of justice; indeed, he had so far ingratiated himself with many former visitors to his country that they would have heard of his capture with feelings of regret. His people, previous to the war, appear to have been quiet and well conducted. It is said that, some time before the outbreak, Kreli had several interviews with Veldtman, the head man of the Fingoes. It is not known with certainty what transpired at these meetings, but it is reported that the object was to secure the alliance of the Fingoes in a war against the whites, and that Kreli even went so far as to offer his daughter in marriage to Veldtman's son; but Veldtman, who for many years held an office under our Government, was most loyal, and, besides, was too sagacious not to see that, if the Europeans were once driven away, the Fingoes at no distant period would become a prey to the overwhelming numbers of the united Amaxosa. As is usual at the advent of a savage war, superstition and imposture were busy: a girl prophesied that all the men who fought on a certain day would be invulnerable, and that they would kill all their enemies; she affirmed that she heard this through the Amahlosi in the voices of the wind and waves, and she took several chiefs to listen to the roaring of the surf on the beaches, and so persuaded them that they fancied they heard the same; the consequence was that, accompanied by the young woman, who was probably the agent of Kreli, they made a furious onslaught on the volunteers and F.A.M.P. (Frontier Armed and Mounted Police). They were severely defeated, and the "witch" herself fell, possibly at the hands of her own people when they discovered how egregiously they had been deceived. The articles in certain newspapers probably contributed to bring about the war by expatiating on the dearth of troops and the inadequate defences of the colony: it was stated in one publication that " a mere handful of ineffective boys," alluding to the F.A.M.P., was the only protection. These and such-like statements were of course read and attentively considered by the educated portions of the Kafir community, who were not slow in publishing their conclusions to their countrymen in general.

The Kafir War.

The war, up to the commencement of December, 1877, was carried on mainly by the volunteers, Fingoes, and F.A.M.P., under Commandant Griffiths, and how completely they performed their work is generally acknowledged. Kreli's kraal was stormed and destroyed, a large proportion of the huts in the country burned, thousands of cattle captured, and the remainder driven by their owners across the Bashee, the colonial forces pursuing as far as the Umtata. The loss to the enemy during this campaign was estimated for me by Commandant Bayly, of the Cape Town Volunteers, one of the most energetic leaders, as follows :—

Gaudana	100
Ibeka	150
The Springs	30
Lusizi	80
Major Elliott's Column	200
'Mtsinzani	100
Capt. Robinson's Engagement	30
Sundries, Skirmishes, &c.	350
	1040

All these things having been achieved, the war was considered at an end, the bulk of the volunteers was disbanded, and they returned to their homes; but the Galekas, immediately ascertaining that our forces had been withdrawn, re-occupied their country. The Gaikas showed a restless disposition, and the aspect of affairs was shortly esteemed so serious that the head-quarters of the 88th regiment was hurried up from Cape Town, a naval brigade from H.M. Flag-ship "Active," with seven guns, was landed at East London on December 16th, more troops were demanded from England, and the volunteers were again hurriedly pushed across the Kei, together with portions of the 1st batt. 24th and 88th regiments. Cattle-stealing became common, not only in the Transkei, but likewise in the colony, which with the Kafirs appears to be tantamount to a declaration of war; but still very many people seemed to believe in the peaceful attitude of the Gaikas. At this juncture I asked a large farmer and an old resident in the Ciskei, whether he thought that the Gaikas would rise. "Sir," he answered, "if the British Government were to send a written declaration of war to Russia, and withdraw its ambassador from St. Petersburg, such acts could not be more unmistakable in their meaning than those of the Gaikas." Yet Sandilli, with the characteristic native cunning, appeared to be on good terms with the Government. At length he became insolent towards the officials, who "interviewed" him for the purpose of ascertaining his intentions; then, as it suited his purpose, apologized; again became insolent; and, at last—Kiva, one of Kreli's chiefs, having crossed the Kei with a force of Galekas—he took to the bush, as most of the old colonists expected from the first that he would. And then the newspapers, from denominating him "the stout Gaika chieftain," spoke of him as "that drunken ruffian,"—an epithet probably deserved.

I may remark that there were two circumstances which certainly contributed to prolong the Kafir war, viz. the complete freedom which we permitted the enemy's women to enjoy, and the liberty which we accorded to the so-called loyal Kafirs. The women spent their days in collecting food and, where possible, ammunition, which they conveyed to the men by night, being intimately acquainted with every path through the bush. They were also invaluable as spies, and in many other ways. It is impossible to starve an enemy into subjection with such a multitudinous and indefatigable commissariat staff. On one occasion a number of women came into our camp carrying fagots for sale: they would take no money in exchange, but only articles of food, such as bread, biscuit, meat, or mealies. They stated that they were Mapassa's people—the name of a neighbouring friendly chief, whom I have previously mentioned; but as they quitted the camp I remarked that they went in a direction exactly contrary to that leading to Mapassa's location, and I called the attention of the officer of the guard to the circumstance, who thereupon, having similar suspicions to my own, directed the remainder to be expelled from the camp. These women unquestionably belonged to the enemy which was holding the bush at no great distance; and their object was, doubtless, partly to ascertain our strength, and partly to procure food for their men. There is a somewhat unjust adage which says, "There is no mischief in the world which has not a woman at the bottom of it;" but this is certainly true as regards the Kafir war, for it is partly the iniquitous system of stealing cattle wherewith to purchase wives, as I have before related, and partly the sneers and taunts of the women at the young men for not being warriors, which are fertile causes of these disturbances. An officer, with a few native troops, attacked a body of Kafirs in a bush, and, shortly putting them to flight, pursued them. Several women, who drew near to view the engagement, ascertaining the smallness of the attacking force, reviled the fugitives, upon which they returned, and cut to pieces the officer and several of his men—the body of the former, when discovered, having no less than seventeen assegai wounds. All the women of a tribe, on the outbreak of a war, should, on pain of death, be made to assemble in a certain part of the country, where they should be fed, and placed under the surveillance of a strong guard, which should permit egress to none.

Restraining the movements of the so-called loyal Kafirs is, I admit, a matter of a more difficult nature; but much might be done to restrict the almost unlimited licence they enjoy. Any Kafir had merely to say that he was loyal, to deliver up any old arms he chose, and to be registered, when he was provided with a printed form or pass, forbidding any one to delay or molest him; and the number of these passes found on the slain, after almost every engagement, testified to the utter inadequacy of such a proceeding.

Moreover, the precautions taken against the treachery of the Kafirs inhabiting the Government reserves in the Transkei were very imperfect. In these reserves numerous petty chiefs reside, who in the aggregate could bring into the field a considerable number of men. During the war a certain English resident, suspecting that all was not right, mustered the Kafirs in the reserve over which he presided. Under ordinary circumstances there should have been upwards of a hundred men, but only some fifteen were forthcoming. It was obvious where the majority of the absentees was; yet any man, who had just before been fighting against us, had merely to return to his reserve, and state that he had been visiting his friends in some distant reserve, or tender any other plausible excuse, to make everything right.

* * * * * *

I have attempted in the foregoing pages to give a brief sketch of the aspect of affairs in Kaffraria which led to the landing of a naval force. At 1 p.m. on December 10th, 1877, H.M.S. "Active," flag-ship of Commodore, now Rear-Admiral, Sir F. W. Sullivan, K.C.B., steamed out of Table Bay, having on board 120 men of the 88th regiment (Connaught

The Kafir War.

Rangers), the hired steamer "Florence" having left a few hours previously with a similar detachment of the same regiment. Just before weighing anchor a telegram had reached Cape Town, stating that a desperate fight had taken place between the Galekas and colonial forces, in which—so ran the telegram—"the latter had to form square and fight for several hours: enemy came within ten yards, answered cheer with cheer, and captured the guard tent." At 7 a.m. on the 13th, the "Active" arrived at East London, the "Florence" coming in soon afterwards—this latter vessel having called on her way at Port Elizabeth, and taken on board the harbour-master, an officer of much experience along the Kaffrarian coast, together with some surf-boats. The commodore soon afterwards went on shore to communicate with Sir Bartle Frere, the Governor, and General Sir A. Cunynghame, commanding the forces, and it was decided that, owing to the critical aspect of affairs, a force composed of some 200 men of H.M.S. "Active" and fifty men of the 88th regt. should be landed at Mazeppa Bay, if possible —a spot about forty miles to the eastward— and there, having formed an entrenched camp, should harass the rear of the enemy as much as possible. On the following day the men of the 88th regt., with the exception of the fifty above mentioned, were embarked in lighters. Shortly afterwards a heavy south-westerly gale came on, so that no landing at East London could be effected. The lighters had to drop anchor in the open sea, where they were violently tossed for upwards of twenty-four hours; they were of course battened down, and in their holds lay, in almost complete darkness, the wretched soldiers, most of them mere boys, exhausted by sea-sickness, without food, water, or air. Occasionally a face, deadly pale, was seen peeping over the bulwarks, and rapidly disappearing as the waves advanced to sweep the decks. During the evening some food was conveyed to them in the life-boat, but the lightermen ate it all, the soldiers being too sick even to look at it. On the 15th a signal was made from the shore that the destination of the naval force was altered— it was to be landed at East London; so, the weather having moderated, six twelve-pounder Armstrongs, two rocket-tubes, and one Gatling gun were at once sent on shore; and on the succeeding morning, Sunday, the undermentioned force from H.M.S. "Active" followed:—Commander H. T. Wright, in command, Lieutenants R. Craigie and W. des V. Hamilton, Lieutenant T. Dowding, R.M.L.I., Sub-Lieutenants A. Loring, R. Cochran, and W. Barnes-Lawrence, Mr. R. Marwood, clerk, Mr. Bays, gunner, and myself, with 121 bluejackets, forty-two marines, and twenty-three Kroomen, forming a total of 196. As we quitted the ship the commodore stood on the poop waving his cap, all the officers and men remaining on board cheered, and the band played "Auld Lang Syne." The formidable bar at the mouth of the Buffalo River, on the right bank of which is situated East London, and on the left Panmure, has to be crossed in capacious lighters, closely fastened down. The atmosphere below soon becomes most offensive and stifling, and on this occasion a few of us determined to encounter what we considered the lesser evil—the chance of the waves on deck. We had just congratulated ourselves on having crossed the bar, when a tremendous sea, curling high above the lighter, broke into her, drenching every one, and very nearly washing one of the lightermen overboard. These lighters are warped across the bar by means of a rope made fast on shore. Judging from the number of inhabitants, including a large proportion of the fair sex, who had assembled to see us land, the clergy of East London must that morning have preached to very scanty congregations. The Kafirs could not understand the blue-jackets, but remarked that "they never saw that sort before," while a burly European vociferously gave it as his opinion that "soldiers were no good—only wait till the sailors get to the front." Our men certainly presented a serviceable appearance, drawn up in a double line, with their white canvas gaiters, rifles, and cutlass bayonets. We were also accompanied by the fifty men of the 88th, under Lieut. Thirkill. Our first halt was to be at Panmure. This rising town, immediately opposite, is built on an elevated site, commanding the most lovely scenery, and here the railway terminus is situated. Our men reached this place after an extremely hot and dusty march of some three miles, the river having been crossed on a floating bridge, warped along by Kafirs. A waggonette, drawn by four grey ponies, was hired from the hotel to convey some of the officers, and whilst it was being got ready we waited in one of the rooms, where two men were smoking, one of whom was

Mr. Yates, who accompanied us as interpreter; he had been associated with the Galekas for years, and was personally acquainted with Kreli. The other had been formerly an officer in the old Cape Mounted Rifles; he was a bronzed man with a dark grizzly beard, who regaled us with stories of his exploits in a former Kafir war: he told me, with seeming infinite enjoyment, that "the Kafirs were all bad shots, and in consequence invariably fired high, and that the tall men were the only ones who ever got hit; indeed, all the men, without exception, that he had ever seen killed were tall men, and that I was certain to fall; he would give nothing for my chance of coming back," &c.; and with the object of impressing this on me, he kindly repeated it two or three times, for which, of course, I felt correspondingly grateful. On our arrival at Panmure we found our tents pitched on a green breezy down, near the railway station, and the little camp all alive with visitors. Among them was a gentleman on horseback, who introduced himself as formerly secretary to a late commodore on this station, but stated that he now resided at Panmure; he invited some of us to dinner and offered the hospitality of his house during our stay, which invitation was very acceptable, as our cooking arrangements were quite in embryo. We found that he kept an extensive general store, which adjoined his residence, where one could purchase anything, from a mouse-trap to a silk dress, and from the top of which floated a large red flag, emblazoned with his name. After dinner our host took us for a pleasant drive to the Kahoon River, about six miles distant; the country was extremely pretty and park-like, covered everywhere with very green grass, and studded with mimosa trees. Jessamine grew wild in some of the kloofs, and the air was redolent of this and other delicious odours. Occasionally we passed hurriedly-constructed huts and tents, in which resided Europeans and their families who had "treked in" from fear of the Kafirs, bringing with them their cattle and household goods, and we encountered several bullock-waggons laden with fresh refugees. The scenery about the Kahoon is bold and picturesque; on each side rises a reddish krantz, crowned by low green hills, all richly wooded. On one of these commanding sites Major Curry has erected a handsome residence, surrounded by an estate of several thousand acres: his house is built of brick, which is a novelty in the neighbourhood, as nearly all the houses in East London and Panmure are constructed of thin corrugated iron or of wood. On the following day, having taken leave of our kind host and of his wife, who had given us a most cordial welcome, we rejoined our force, and left Panmure by a special train soon after mid-day, for the Kei Road Station, some forty-four miles distant, from whence we were to commence our march for the front. There was tremendous cheering as we steamed out of the station, and all along the line; as we passed the little groups of white people engaged in agriculture, they ceased to work and cheered heartily. For the first thirty miles the country was undulating, grassy, and open, and as our gunnery lieutenant kept remarking, "a splendid country for artillery," sprinkled as is the greater part of South Africa with Kafir kraals and mimosa trees. For the remainder of the journey we ran parallel to the Amatola Mountains, where the Buffalo River rises, and here the country became much more hilly.

On our arrival at the Kei Road Station we found that it was held by a detachment of the 1st batt. 24th, under Lieut. Atkinson, and a company of local volunteers, in all kinds of attire: they reminded me of Falstaff's regiment, although well armed with Snider rifles and bayonets. They seemed to consider a Gaika rising imminent, and every available man was evidently under arms, for among them was a little antiquated individual with a wooden leg drilling away most perseveringly. We found that our baggage, with the guns, had already arrived, but that our tents had been left behind at Panmure; so the men were housed for the night in the goods shed, and the officers in one of the waiting-rooms. We made a comfortable dinner at Heath's Hotel, a building about half a mile away, which, together with a couple of stores, constituted the place, which rejoiced in the name of "Hangman's Bush." Here also were numerous huts, crammed with refugees. Close to the hotel was a camp of the F.A.M.P., which force patrolled the neighbourhood; there was likewise a detachment of the Queenstown Volunteer Horse, which had escorted several ammunition waggons from King William's Town. The next day our tents arrived, and our camp soon presented a very respectable appearance. In the afternoon, the Naval Brigade was inspected by Sir B. Frere and Gen. Sir A. Cunynghame, both of whom had come from King William's Town for the purpose. After the inspection the general delivered a speech, in which he stated that "he had never inspected a finer body of men, that he had never been more pleased in all his long experience, that when he had served in the trenches before Sebastopol he numbered among his dearest friends certain officers of the Naval Brigade, and that he would do everything for us that lay in his military power." The evolutions with the Armstrong guns and the Gatling caused a marked sensation among the Kafir lookers-on. The latter is fired by turning a handle round and round, and they went away with the idea that it was "a machine for grinding up Kafirs." On the 19th, four horses arrived for Capt. Wright, Lieut. Craigie, Mr. Marwood, and myself; and at 2 p.m., all our tents, guns, and baggage having been placed on bullock-waggons, we marched in the direction of the River Kei. Our waggons were thirty in number, and our force consisted, besides the Naval Brigade, of about 150 men of the 88th. Towards evening, having crossed the Gonubi River, where some of the waggons stuck, and were extricated with much difficulty, we encamped by moonlight on a plateau above the river, the long dry grass making excellent beds, and our horses being made fast to the trunks of the trees. On our route we generally turned out at 4 a.m., bathed in the river or stream, near which we had encamped or bivouacked, partook of some biscuit and cocoa, and commenced our march about 5.30 a.m. Immediately that we had vacated our camping grounds they were generally overrun by numbers of Kafir women and children, who diligently searched the long grass, and screamed with delight on finding a piece of candle, biscuit, or a few mealies which the horses had left. As we were quitting the Gonubi, a despatch arrived to say that our force was to be divided, Lieut. Craigie, Sub-Lieut. Barnes-Lawrence, Mr. Bays, gunner, and 100 men, with two guns, were to march to Fort Cunynghame, a place about twenty-five miles distant, at the foot of the Amatolas, where they were to act as a garrison. When we had proceeded a short distance this force took a road which branched away to the left: we gave them three cheers as they departed, but they appeared too crestfallen to return them, for they regarded themselves "shelved," as they termed it, while they looked on us as about to enjoy to the full the excitement of war. As we passed along the country we found all the European residences deserted. The weather was intensely hot, and we halted for ten minutes in every hour. We arrived about noon at Dribosch, where there was a very fair hotel, kept by an European, and in a valley close by a detachment of the 88th had outspanned. The space around this hotel was crowded with Kafirs of both sexes, evidently attracted by curiosity; they belonged to the chief Dimba, whose kraal was not far distant. Here we had an excellent luncheon, the waitress being a Gaika in European dress, and as pert a young woman as I ever met. One of our officers, who possessed considerable powers of bantering, attempted to " chaff" her, but her answers were too much even for him, and he soon had to desist from his attempt. After luncheon we continued our march to Komgha, across a poor barren country, sparsely covered with long, thin, dry grass and destitute of trees. The heat was insufferable; clouds of black dust enveloped us; all the water-bottles were soon emptied, and could not be replenished; and on our arrival at that place, with our faces blistered, and so coated with the horrible black dust, that we resembled a corps of Kafirs. The men rushed up to the first building they saw, and begged a drink of water, "for God's sake." Komgha is a place of some size, possessing two very good hotels, and three or four large general stores, in which almost anything may be bought; and there is a never-failing supply of good water. Most of the houses were surrounded by a double wall of planking about six feet in height, filled in between with earth, and loop-holed; this had been done by direction of the authorities, in view of the threatened Gaika rising. Numerous Europeans, with their families and goods, had fled thither, and were living in sheds or tents, and the surrounding country was covered with their cattle, which were regularly driven in at sunset. Near our camp was a barrack of the F.A.M.P.: we found that the low walls which surrounded it had been heightened by means of bags of earth, and loop-holed for musketry. Their videttes were also stationed about the adjacent country, so as to form a cordon around Komgha, and bring in immediate intelligence of any suspicious movement among the natives. In the barracks were some ninety troopers. Whilst here, we heard that Botman, one of Kreli's principal councillors, had surrendered to the military in the Transkei. We left behind us at Komgha two Armstrongs and the Gatling gun, with ten seamen gunners, for the further protection of the place. About half-way between Komgha and the Kei we halted at a large house occupied by a Mr. Pullen, who owned a farm of some 4000 acres, principally grazing land. We found that this place had recently been put into a complete state of defence by Lieut. Anstey, of the 24th regt. It was tenanted by the families of several of the neighbouring farmers, while close by were encamped fifty men of the 88th, under Lieut. Moore. Here the descent of the Kei Valley commences, and the aspect of the country changes; one looks down upon several high table-lands with precipitous sides, all the extensive intervening valleys being rocky and densely wooded; the hill-sides are also in many places umbrageous with bush, in others studded with immense numbers of dry-looking stumpy aloes. We continued to descend by a winding road for about five miles, raising dense clouds of white dust as we proceeded. The men amused themselves by singing, adapting certain popular songs to their present circumstances, the principal being, "We'll hang old Kreli (which they pronounced Kree-loy) on a sour apple tree," and "In Kreli's country over there," pointing to the scene beyond the river. As we approached the Kei we lost the mountain breezes, and the heat became much more oppressive. A short distance from the right bank we passed a small encampment of the F.A.M.P., which was placed there to prevent any Kafirs taking possession of the drift, or destroying the bridge. This bridge across the Kei was a long wooden structure, sufficiently wide for horsemen to pass singly, but the foundations of a much finer and more durable one were being laid. The river was low, but its broad stony bed showed that during the rains it conveys to the sea an immense volume of water; it is thickly wooded on either side. About two miles further up was a lofty headland known as Murderer's Kop, so named from the circumstance that, during a former Kafir war, a few army officers, who were encamped in the neighbourhood, foolishly made an excursion to this place. A large force of Kafirs suddenly surrounded and attacked them; they fought most valiantly, but were eventually killed and their bodies thrown over the precipice. Crossing the drift was no easy matter. I rode through the turbid water for a distance of some two hundred yards, the bottom evidently consisting of numerous boulders; my horse crept carefully through, constantly stumbling and reeling, so that I expected momentarily to alight in the water: at one place I observed a large snake swimming past me. As we reached the opposite side, one of our marines fell in the ooze: he burst into a violent rage, and exclaimed, as he arose, covered with mud, "I'll corpse every Kafir in the country after this!"

Several hours were occupied in getting the waggons across. As soon as the first arrived, which carried the tents, we encamped in a small open space in the bush, close to the river: it was a bad situation for a camp, as we might have been advantageously attacked on three sides under cover of the darkness, but there was no other. Our sentries were doubled, and had particular orders to watch the ground, so that no Kafirs could creep on them with their assegais—formerly a favourite practice of theirs—their half-hourly calls of "All's well" during the night sounding very peculiar coming from among the bushes. As we ascended into the country on the left bank of the Kei, the heat surpassed everything I ever before experienced; it became so great that the oxen were speedily exhausted, and we were compelled to outspan; awnings were spread between the waggons for the men, and a tent was pitched for the officers. Our halting-place was a broad table-land about five hundred feet above the river; the northwest wind swept over us like the blasts of a furnace, and laden with sand; the thermometer in the shade stood at 116.° Every drop of water we possessed was speedily consumed, and we lent our horses to the men to go down to the river and bring up more. The ground on which we sat was scorching, our lips were blistered, and the cuticle peeled from our hands and faces; two of our men became insensible from heat apoplexy. We procured a tin of preserved meat and some rum from our commissariat waggon: I happened to possess a bottle of pickles, and another officer contributed a bottle of milk, which, mixed with a small quantity of rum, revived us very much. As we were making our meal we were joined by an old man who was travelling in a waggon in the contrary direction, and had halted at the same spot. He informed us that he was on the way to visit his son at King William's Town, or "King" as it is familiarly styled in the colony; he had fought in the old Kafir wars, and his anecdotes were of such a nature as certainly did not become a man of his years. He regaled himself liberally on our rum and beef, and as he left asked for the remainder of the pickles; and out of gratitude he gave us what he termed a "tip" on parting, which was this: "when we got to the front, never to eat or drink anything offered us by a Kafir, as it was sure to be poisoned." Late in the afternoon, the wind having shifted, we pursued our journey, but with much difficulty, as the road wound round steep hills and the oxen seemed weak. The scenery was grand in the extreme, and I was sorry when night hid it from our view. From the high lands the windings of the Kei could be traced for miles, sometimes disappearing through dark rocky gorges; then, suddenly shining forth like a broad band of burnished silver, it gradually became less distinct, until it seemed to be absorbed into the soft blueness of some distant mountains. The valley through which it ran appeared to average about two miles in breadth, and was covered with trees and rushes; it was bounded generally by reddish krantzes, some of which must have been several hundred feet in height. We were joined on the road by Lieut. Curran of the 88th, who was to accompany us as staff-officer. We reached Tolene, in the Fingo country, about midnight, and there found an hotel, but it was closed, and the sentries round the camp seemed to have disappeared, for, although we rode close up to the tents, no one challenged us. Every one was very tired, and, rolling ourselves in our great coats on the ground, we slept soundly. The next morning the reveillé sounded at 3 a.m., and we started for Butterworth. I felt much fatigued, and, happening to fall asleep on my horse, narrowly escaped a fall. The country we passed through was thickly populated by Fingoes. We rode up to several kraals and bought fowls at a shilling each, and eggs twenty-four for a shilling, the owners indulging in long consultations before they let them go. Butterworth is situated close to a small river. There are a few European houses, the best of which is occupied by the Rev. Mr. Warner, a Wesleyan clergyman, whose church was close to his residence; there is a large store, a wine merchant's establishment, and great numbers of Fingo huts, which not only fringe the summits of the hills surrounding the place, but also occupy the major portions of the sides; indeed, the Fingo population of Butterworth must be considerable. We marched from here early on the morning of Christmas Day, *en route* to Ibeka, the head-quarters of the Transke field force, seven miles distant. Soon afterwards we passed the house of an European, quite deserted; the owner must have taken his departure very suddenly, as his cash account book lay open on the table. Our men helped themselves pretty freely to the coal, which was scattered all over the place, to cook their Christmas dinners, which were to consist of a lot of geese they had bought at Butterworth, and which they busied themselves with picking as they marched. As we proceeded we very shortly got into the Galeka territory, as was evident from the numerous charred circles marking the sites of the huts which had been burned by the Fingoes. Here there was a second deserted European house, which seemed to have been wrecked, and the owner of which must have been either a wag or a fool, as he had placed "To let" in one of the windows. We ascended a very steep and rugged hill, and saw on the distant horizon a row of trees looking like poplars; this was a line of blue gums (*Eucalyptus globulus*), which, with a trader's store-house surrounded by a large number of tents, represented Ibeka. After advancing about a mile further, we remarked at some distance to our left a long, low, white house, with numerous kraals in the neighbourhood; this was the residence of Veldtman, head man of the Fingoes. On reaching Ibeka we found that the camp contained parts of the 1st batt. 24th and 88th regts., Volunteers, and F.A.M.P., under the command of Col. Glyn. We were loudly cheered as we marched into the camp, and our tents were soon pitched on a hill close by. There was an officers' mess-tent near, and we were kindly invited there to breakfast by Major Logan and Surgeon-Major Cuffe.

As it was Christmas Day, the officers of the Naval Brigade all dined together, the *menu* comprising soup, a cold turkey, and a plum pudding; the latter, which was the handiwork of one of our officers, was rather a failure, as all the raisins were at the bottom, which, besides, was very much burned; however, the upper parts were very good after having been set on fire with rum, and then eaten with a pot of strawberry jam procured from the trader's store. The turkey was originally purchased at the Kei Road railway station: it travelled as far as Komgha on the limber of the Gatling gun, afterwards on one of the waggons, and at night it was always tied by the leg to one of the tent-pegs and fattened on mealies.

Gen. Sir A. Cunynghame, accompanied by Sub-Lieut. Loring, of H.M.S. "Active," Naval A.D.C., arrived towards evening, also a small party of Royal Artillery, with two guns from St. Helena, under the command of Lieut. Kell, 88th regt. Kreli was said to be within a few miles of Ibeka with a considerable force, but to be sueing for peace: whether he would procure it on the terms he wished was considered very doubtful. About fifty Galekas came in and surrendered. The general reviewed all the regular forces in camp on the following day, among which was a troop of mounted infantry, under Lieut. Clements of the 24th, after which he delivered a long complimentary speech. We were subsequently informed that two columns would leave Ibeka on the following day, one of which, the larger, under Col. Glyn, was to scour the country towards the Quora River; and of this a body of our blue-jackets, with a rocket-tube, was to form part; it was to be the head-quarter and central column, which Capt. Wright, R.N., accompanied, and of which I was placed in medical charge. The second, or left column, under Capt. Upcher of the 24th, with which our marines were incorporated, was to operate beyond the Quora; while a third, or right column, was already in the field, between the Kei and Quora, commanded by Major Hopton of the 88th. There was a camp under Capt. Robinson, R.A., some fifteen miles away, which was to be the extent of our first day's journey, and here we were to receive reinforcements before proceeding further. Not a kraal was to be seen along the line of march, but their former sites were everywhere marked by a ring of black circles on the ground, with the partially destroyed hurdle-work in the centre. From all along the distant hills rose dense columns of smoke, showing that detachments of Fingoes were actively at work. On arriving at our destination we found the camp occupied by the artillery division of the F.A.M.P., and close by was a large Fingo encampment of temporary huts, formed from the branches of trees and covered with long grass. I here met Mr. Allan Maclean, the

The Kafir War. 107

most energetic of the three brothers of that name, all of whom have rendered themselves famous as Fingo leaders, also Commandant Gray, who so ably led the Volunteers at that hotly-contested engagement "the Springs," and other fighting celebrities. On leaving this camp our column consisted of 50 Naval Brigade, 125 F.A.M.P., with 2 seven-pounder guns, 150 of the 24th regt., and 1500 Fingoes, forming a total of 1825. Our route lay along mountain ridges commanding a distant view of the sea and connected by narrow necks of land, the sides of which were thickly wooded and covered with long tambooki grass, from whence small numbers of Kafirs might have attacked us with great advantage. The usual plan of campaigning in this country is to strike the tents in the early morning as soon as it is sufficiently light, to make a "trek" of some miles, then to outspan and give the oxen at least two hour's grazing, and unsaddle the horses, knee-halter, and turn them out to feed, surrounded by a guard; to let the men cook and eat a meal; then make another "trek," and encamp or bivouac late in the afternoon, so as to allow plenty of grazing time for the oxen before dark. It will thus be seen that marching in company with bullock waggons is necessarily slow and tedious, and allows plenty of time for the enemy to avoid a force whenever he may wish. Lieut. Cochrane, of the artillery division of the F.A.M.P., kindly invited me to share his meal at our first outspan. I was surprised at the celerity exhibited by the troopers of that force on such an occasion—of course acquired by constant practice; they would dismount, unsaddle, knee-halter, light a fire, and have water boiled within ten minutes. Our cavalry scoured the open country and the Fingoes traversed the bush without finding any Kafirs.

On our road we passed the site of a recent battle between our forces and the Galekas; among the slain were two valiant brothers, Englishmen, called Goss. Further on we encamped on an elevated ground called Luzisi, within a few miles of the Quora River; and shortly afterwards the Fingoes came pouring in, under Veldtman. All were armed with a gun and a bundle of assegais, and wore European clothes, with a bright red handkerchief fastened round the hat as a distinguishing badge. These men continued to rendezvous at our camp during the greater part of the night. We had not proceeded far on the

The Kafir War.

following day, a large body of Fingoes having pushed on in front, before we suddenly heard heavy firing. The artillery, with their guns, and the blue-jackets, with their rocket tube, were ordered rapidly forward, and I cantered on with them. I soon found that a brisk fight was going on among some kraals situated on the side of a hill immediately above one of the drifts of the Quora. The enemy was soon driven down a ravine and across the drift, vigorously pursued by the Fingoes; a large number of women and children came streaming up to the top of the hill, and, as soon as it was ascertained that the huts were empty, all the kraals were set on fire. It appeared also that the left column, to which our marines were attached, must have reached the country opposite, as columns of smoke from the burning kraals were springing up on all the distant hills. The Fingoes searched the bags of all the women and took away everything of value they possessed. I saw one man's finger covered with rings, which he had just removed from a handsome leopard-skin bag. Shortly after that the Kafirs had gained the opposite side of the river, they were reinforced by large numbers of their countrymen, who were evidently guarding the cattle which were grazing beyond; however, the Fingoes swarmed across after them, and a smart action ensued, which lasted for some three hours, when the Galekas retired precipitately in all directions through the Quora bush. The European troops took up a position so as to oppose them should they attempt to recross the river at a drift lower down, or to cut them off should they retreat along the opposite bank; the guns were also laid so as to command a ravine it was thought they might occupy, but in which we were mistaken. Close to the kraals I passed the body of a Galeka which had been shot through the lungs. The Fingoes are evidently excellent skirmishers; they took advantage of every stone, or tree, or clump of grass which would afford the slightest cover as they pushed boldly forward; nothing will, however, stop a Fingo where there are any cattle to be got, and their eyesight is wonderful. They were seen gradually surrounding the cattle and driving them towards one spot, where they were protected by a strong guard. Their greed for cattle is surprising: during the action I noticed one man, evidently of a pacific nature, suddenly jump up and rush by me with eyes as if about to start from his head. I asked him where he was going: he would not stop, but shouted "Cattle, master, cattle," at the same time pointing in a particular direction. I could see nothing, but on directing my field-glass towards the spot I perceived a large number which he had evidently just discovered. That evening 910 head of cattle were driven into our camp, besides a large flock of goats. Such captures as these have more effect in subduing the Galekas than anything else; indeed, it is the only loss which makes any decided impression upon them. All these cattle were distributed among the Fingoes, and driven back to their country by a sufficient escort. Our next step was to search the Manubi forest, a place some five miles in length by two in breadth. The Fingoes set out some hours earlier and gained the western end, whilst the European troops occupied the eastern, so as suddenly to fall on the enemy while retreating before the Fingoes. We burned a large number of kraals as we marched towards the forest, most of which had been very recently occupied. The wisdom of this proceeding was questionable, as it was the smoke from them that probably showed the enemy our route, and caused him to avoid us. When we reached the forest, through which there was a tolerable road, we halted for a long time among some magnificent trees, waiting to attack a foe which never came. The Fingoes killed several Galekas in the forest and captured a number of cattle, but the main body evidently got away in some other direction. Beyond this we approached the sandy shores of Mazeppa Bay, and then came to the mouth of the Quora, where we encamped on a small grassy plain close to the sea. On our arrival a fine buck started from the ground: half a dozen rifles were discharged at it, but the animal escaped. We had to remain here a day in order to construct a bridge across the river for our waggons, the pontoons for which arrived on other waggons from Ibeka under a strong guard commanded by Capt. Nixon, R.E. The blue-jackets were quite at home at this work, two of them swimming the river with the ends of the ropes in their teeth, and they soon put the bridge together; while a large party of men was employed in cutting down brushwood to lay on the large sandy tract which intervened between our camp and the river, so as to form a firm road for the passage of the waggons. The beach, which consisted of beautiful silver sand, was strewed with the huge trunks and branches of trees, which had evidently been carried down from the forests by the Quora, when swollen by heavy rains, and afterwards thrown up by the waves. There is a most extensive oyster-bed at the mouth of the Quora, and at low water I went in with my clasp knife and surprised these mollusks. When their shells were separated, I never tasted more delicious oysters in Europe. As the tide rose, I employed a Fingo, who first collected a number and then opened them with his assegai. Rock oysters are also plentiful all along the coast, but these are of far inferior flavour. Whilst here we heard that desperate engagements had taken place between the Gaikas and some of the F.A.M.P. and 88th regiment near Komgha, and that the hotel at Dribosch, where we had luncheon, had been burned by the enemy a few days afterwards. Our Fingoes had evidently heard of the Gaika rising, and were gradually deserting, doubtless hurrying back to their country to defend their homes and the numerous cattle which they have acquired: sixty men disappeared in a few hours. Two of our blue-jackets captured a Galeka crouching behind some rocks not far from the camp, some half-dozen more, who were also concealed, running away into the bush: it is wonderful how stealthily they creep about. We also received intelligence that Major Elliott, with his force of Tembus, had been having a series of skirmishes between the Quora and Bashee, killing some seventy of the enemy, and losing only a very few of his own men and a trooper of the F.A.M.P.

On the first day of the new year, the pontoon bridge being complete, we made the passage of the river and shaped our course for the Jujuga. We had observed for some time H.M.S. "Active" cruising in the distance. On seeing our column she neared the shore and sent two boats to communicate; but all attempts were rendered futile by the surf, and we were only able to exchange signals. Having arrived at the right bank of the Jujuga, we sent horsemen in every direction to discover a ford, but without success. All the waggons were consequently brought to a halt, and Col. Glyn, finding the progress of the column delayed by so many obstacles, rightly conjectured that he would never come up with the Kafirs under such circumstances; so he ordered Maclean's

The Kafir War.

Fingoes, about 1100 strong, to proceed onwards immediately, and, leaving the waggons and infantry to rendezvous near Malan's mission station, he determined to make a rapid movement, with all the cavalry he could muster, on the Udwessa Forest, near the Bashee, where the enemy was reported to be in force. Whilst we were halting here, Lieut. Dowding, who commanded our marines, and some other officers of the left column, which had also arrived within a short distance, rode over and joined us. They informed us that their force had burned a large number of kraals, had taken about a hundred Galeka prisoners and killed many more, besides capturing about 500 head of cattle.

The force which started for the Udwessa consisted of 120 men and two guns of the F.A.M.P., and ninety mounted infantry. Col. Glyn himself took the command, and it was accompanied by Capt. Wright and myself. After riding some twenty miles we came to the outskirts of the Udwessa, and here saw our Fingoes, drawn up in companies, in a lofty position, towards the sea. Maclean rode down and told us that they had searched the forests, but that the bulk of the enemy had vacated it, and had, together with their cattle, crossed the Bashee into the Bomvana country. They had not passed over scatheless, however, as the "Active" had been on the watch and had fired some shell into them from her six-and-a-half ton guns. The natives, who occupied some extensive kraals just across the river, on seeing the ship, had rushed down to the beach, brandishing their weapons, but a well-pitched shell had sent them flying to the bush with great precipitation. The commodore would not destroy the kraals, as he was afraid they might contain women or children. Col. Glyn wished to communicate with the commodore, and Capt. Wright very gallantly volunteered to proceed to the mouth of the Bashee, attended by only a few Fingoes; and by these a letter was also sent to Mr. Fynn, our Resident among the Bomvanas, requesting him to meet us at Malan's mission station and bring one of the sons of Moni (chief of the Bomvanas) with him. We then set out on our return. The road for a long distance lay through a difficult bush, where there was only a very rudimentary footpath: some of the hills were very steep, and we were all obliged to dismount and drag our horses after us beneath the branches. Before entering the

The Kafir War.

bush every man was ordered to load his rifle, and the officers went revolver in hand, for a very small force of the enemy in such a place might have done considerable damage. When we had penetrated for a long distance, we came to a place where the Kafirs had been very recently slaughtering cattle, as several fresh hides were lying about. A short distance beyond we heard a rifle-shot: this was from our interpreter, who, hearing Kafirs' voices, immediately fired in their direction, when four women appeared. They were questioned as to the whereabouts of the men, but of course lied, as they said they had seen none for a month. Our interpreter declared that nothing short of threatening to shoot them, or something of that kind, was likely to elicit the truth, but this suggestion was not acted on. A little further on we met two Galeka men holding out a dirty rag on a stick, which they intended as a flag of truce. The questions put to them were satisfactorily answered, and as they were unarmed, and gave assurances of their neutrality in the war, they were not molested. When we emerged from the bush we passed the corpses of two Kafirs; one had a goat-skin bag by his side, which contained a flint, steel, tobacco, and two knives of English manufacture; the other had been shot through the back of the head : his red blanket was lying at a little distance, which he had evidently thrown off, so as to fly more quickly from his pursuers. The nights were very cold and wet, and it was very unpleasant sleeping in the rain, for we had no tents; and, on rising, the ground beneath us was often converted into a kind of swamp. On one occasion we made a large fire and lay round it, when a very young calf and a little kid, which had evidently been lost, came bleating out of a wood: they advanced to the fire to warm themselves, and took our noses and the lobes of our ears in their mouths and sucked at them, thinking they were with their mothers. The Fingoes, who were bivouacking near, set the whole adjacent country on fire. It was grand after dark to see the flaming of the long dry grass and to hear the incessant crackling of the burning trees and bushes. As we marched back we captured numerous cattle, their owners flying with all speed ; we were also reinforced by 300 mounted Tembus under Major Boyes, an old cavalry officer and one of our Residents among that tribe. He informed us that the Gaika rising had assumed serious proportions, and that several soldiers of the 88th had been killed. We arrived subsequently on the summit of a broad low hill: the surrounding kloofs were well wooded, and contained excellent water. Here were the ruins of two houses, some time before plundered and burned by the Galekas: one of them had evidently been used as a church, as close to it remained a bell fastened to the top of a pole. This was the mission station of Major Malan, who was very assiduous in his efforts to convert the Galekas: judging by the remains of the burnt kraals around, the district must have been populous. A short distance beyond this place we encamped, having been joined by the waggons and infantry of our own and also of the left column, which columns were now broken up; part was to push on to the Bashee mouth, part to form an earthwork at Malan's mission, while the Naval Brigade was ordered to return to Ibeka, about twenty-two miles distant. We found, on arrival, that this place had been put into a complete state of defence; earthworks had been thrown up around the camp, and guns mounted. The Gaikas were reported to be committing all kinds of outrages beyond the Kei, and nightly from the heights of Ibeka could be seen fires caused by the burning of farm and other houses; a party of them had also passed the Kei, near the drift, and burned several Fingo kraals. A few days afterwards Capt. Wright returned to Ibeka from his journey to the mouth of the Bashee to communicate with the "Active;" he was accompanied by Lieut. E. Davis of that ship. It appeared that the boat sent from the "Active" had capsized in the surf. One of the crew, named Daffey, a signal-man, had been drowned, and Davis, with the remainder, narrowly escaped a similar fate, having succeeded, after almost superhuman efforts, in reaching the shore, when clothes and provisions were floated to them in barrels from the ship. We were glad to see our old messmate again, and to congratulate him on his escape. We learnt that a short time ago the "Active," having anchored off a part of the coast known as Bowker's Bay, sent a boat to try if a landing could be effected; a large body of armed Kafirs came down to offer resistance, when the commodore opened fire with shell, which sent them flying to the bush: it was reported that a number were killed. It is not very pleasant sleeping on the ground: even in this camp a night adder was killed in the next tent to mine, and a cobra a short

The Kafir War.

distance off, besides which a man found a snake between his blankets just as he was about to lie down.

On January 13th news came that Kiva, with the Galeka force, which some time ago crossed the Kei to effect a junction with Sandilli, had recrossed it near Mapassa's territory, reinforced by a large following of Gaikas, and that they were in the vicinity of the right column, now commanded by Major Owen of the 88th. Forming part of Owen's force was a company of our blue-jackets, with a 24-pounder rocket-tube, under Sub-Lieut. Cochran. As it was considered judicious to send reinforcements with all despatch, Col. Glyn immediately started with a fresh column, including our marines, under Lieut. Dowding, in the direction of the Quintana Mountain. The same evening the enemy, some 2000 strong, boldly attacked Major Owen's column, at a place called 'Nyamaka, trying to outflank him; when Col. Glyn's column, hurrying on, took part in the engagement, effectually preventing this manœuvre. The enemy fought stubbornly and pluckily, but were soon completely routed, losing about fifty killed; while, on our side, one Fingo and four soldiers of the 88th were wounded

—two of them, however, very severely. Cochran's rockets did good service, causing both consternation and destruction among the Kafirs, and more than one body was afterwards found completely split in two by these missiles, so accurately were they directed. Major Owen behaved very gallantly in this affair, making great personal endeavours to remove the wounded from under a heavy fire. The blue-jackets seemed to enter into this action with feelings of enjoyment; after its conclusion, one of them was heard to remark, "Them ere chaps couldn't ha' done it better if they'd tried—to be so obligin' as to come nice and 'andy to the camp, so that we could go and 'av a jolly good row, and then jest walk in and 'av a feed!"

Two days subsequently, a considerable body of our troops marched to the extensive bush near the Kei, which was searched for the beaten enemy, but only a very few of them were seen. Major Owen's column now marched parallel to the Kei, so that we might attack any bodies of Kafirs which might be lurking in the bush. After journeying some four miles we entered Mapassa's territory: his people had received peremptory orders to leave the vicinity of the Kei the next day, for although they professed loyalty to us, they were strongly suspected of conniving at the crossing of the Gaikas; any cattle found after to-morrow were to be confiscated, any men were to be shot. We consequently saw large numbers of his people with their cattle "treking" eastward. Mapassa asked, some time since, that we would place an English Resident with him: this official came to meet us and conduct us through his territory. We burned all his kraals which were on our line of march, to give him a hint to clear out, and to convince him that we were in earnest. We found all his men drawn up in several divisions, each bearing a large white flag, with the words "Mapassa No. 1," "Mapassa No. 2," and so on, in black letters. The women, who were nearly all profusely ornamented with red clay, offered our men milk, and they were allowed to halt for a short time to drink it. At a neighbouring drift of the Kei, Mapassa maintained a well-armed force, to oppose any attempts which the Gaikas might make to invade his territory. We continued our march to the "Ebb and Flow" drift, about three or four miles above the mouth of the Kei. Our guide was a Fingo, who prided himself on his knowledge of the country, and, of course, took us in the wrong direction; so we had to return a distance of several miles, the unfortunate Fingo being all the time the object of general execration. We eventually encamped near the drift, but our men, in passing some hours before, had fired the Veldt, so they had now to beat out the line of burning grass with branches before we could pitch our tents. The edge of the fire was lined with numbers of large locust birds, which, singular to relate, appeared perfectly conscious that the advancing flames would drive all the locusts in their direction. Our orders were to rise at 3.30 the next morning, so as to be at the drift by daybreak, as numerous cattle had been seen by one of our reconnoitring parties in that neighbourhood. About midnight a sergeant awoke me and said that he wanted to lower my tent, as all the others had been down for the last five minutes. I looked out and found that the entire camp had disappeared, and that all the men were lying on the grass under arms, while everything was as silent as the grave. The reason was that shots had been heard a short distance off, and it was supposed that the enemy was surrounding us in force, under cover of the darkness, and was about to make an attack on our camp. I seized my revolver, and, when my tent was lowered, I lay down and partly covered myself with some of the canvas, as it had come on to rain. We lay on the ground for some time awaiting the Kafir onset, and I thought how advantageously we might, in a war with savages, take a lesson from the ancient Romans. Here was a camp without any obstacle to impede the progress of an enemy, and without any cover for the defenders, who, moreover, standing against the sky-line, would present a much better mark to the enemy than he, advancing in the darkness up the hill, would to them. The old Roman forces never, under any circumstances, encamped for a night without surrounding themselves with a ditch and earthwork. In Cæsar, we read that when he fought with the savages of Gaul, which was much the same kind of warfare as that in which we were now engaged, how persistently he kept part of his army under arms until the remainder had fortified the camp. The worst of it was that the surrounding country was so generally blackened, owing to the Veldt having been fired, that had the whole Kafir army been close to us we could not have seen it. There was something very weird about the scene: occasionally a shot was heard, and then the lowing of cattle. We now concluded that the Kafirs, having discovered our plans, were driving off their cattle; consequently, two Fingo horsemen were sent away to reconnoitre, but they shortly returned, saying they could see nothing.

We were at the drift by 4 a.m., and, having been joined by 300 Fingoes, immediately crossed the Kei into the colony, and scoured the adjacent country, our European force consisting of part of the Naval Brigade, with a rocket-tube, detachments of the 24th and 88th regiments, and some artillery with two seven-pounder guns. The rockets and shells were admirably directed, bursting exactly in the right spots. A number of Gaikas were killed, as they defended their cattle with much pertinacity. When put to flight, the Fingo Horse pursued with great alacrity, and brought in 430 horned cattle, and about 850 sheep and goats. The price of an ordinary bullock is about three pounds, that of a sheep fifteen shillings; and as the columns operating beyond the Kei are reported to have lately captured 4000 of the former, such losses cannot be without their effect on the enemy, although many cattle possessed by the Gaikas have been stolen from Europeans. The Fingoes did not seem to care for anything but the horned cattle; the white occupants of each tent, therefore, selected a couple of sheep, which were soon killed, flayed, and suspended from poles opposite the tent doors, so that each man might select what parts he liked; the remainder were allowed to wander wherever they liked, and probably fell into the hands of Mapassa's people. We discovered subsequently that our night alarm was caused by Maclean's Fingoes, who were returning to Col. Glyn's camp in the distance with a large drove of captured cattle, and the shots were fired occasionally to frighten away any Kafirs who might be contemplating a rescue.

As we continued our march, we passed the remains of a house which had been plundered and then set on fire; this was known as "Crouch's shop," and was not long since a general store, kept by a trader of that name. We then passed through a district covered with ant-hills, and, after fording the Kologha River at its mouth, journeyed along the sea-beach for above a mile; and four miles further on crossed the Kobinaba, at a very rugged drift, with steep declivities on either side, which the waggons were some two hours in passing; so I rode on, unsaddled and knee-haltered my horse, and turned him into a mealie field in which several other horses were likewise revelling. I then strolled through a large garden, close to which a kraal had been burned, and regaled myself with blackberries and Cape gooseberries, which I was glad to get, as we had had very little fresh vegetable food of late. We bivouacked towards evening on a grassy slope above a stream; there was a wood opposite, and close to it were seen three armed Kafirs. An officer of the F.A.M.P., who was foremost, immediately brought one down with his rifle, the others fled into the wood: the body looked half starved, and the mouth contained some mealies, which, perhaps, the man had recently the good fortune to discover. These men were probably either spies sent to watch our movements, or else were on a foraging expedition from the main body. There were several burned kraals in this neighbourhood, but all the mealie pits had been opened and their contents removed, probably the work of the volunteers and Fingoes during the first stage of the war. Before prosecuting our march, a patrol of the F.A.M.P., with some Fingoes, was sent to examine the outskirts of the Manubi forest, from which we were not far distant, in order to ascertain if there were any recent spoors of the enemy, so that we might attack them if present. This reconnaissance discovered a few Galekas and cattle beyond the Quora, but none in the forest. I rode for some miles by the side of Veldtman, who gave me a great deal of information as to the country and people; he told me that some of the more important Galeka chiefs owned from 500 to 1000 head of cattle, worth from 3*l*. to 8*l*. each; that Kreli possessed very large numbers—he did not, however, keep them all in the vicinity of his kraal, but divided them into small bodies, and parcelled them out among his subjects for pasturage, they being allowed to appropriate the milk by way of compensation. Shortly afterwards a rather amusing incident occurred. On rounding a hill, we saw several men who looked like armed Kafirs driving a few cattle across a valley a short distance from us; two troopers of the F.A.M.P. and half-a-dozen Fingoes were ordered to take them; these, on getting within range, opened fire, upon which the supposed Kafirs, throwing away their assegais, took to their heels and disappeared in the bush, leaving ten bullocks, which were immediately captured. We soon, however, discovered that these were some slaughter oxen sent on to us by the Commissariat at Ibeka, and the drivers, not supposing that we should have marched so quickly, were making a short cut across country to intercept us, so that we had been capturing our own cattle; it was, however, fortunate that none of the drivers were injured. After a very long and fatiguing march we encamped in the evening on the battle-field of 'Mtsinzani. Here, on an elevated site, was a hastily constructed earthwork, thrown up by the colonial volunteers, under Captain Bayly, who commanded in this action, wherein a small number of men successfully held their position against an overwhelming force of Kafirs, until reinforced from Ibeka. This fight took place less than two months before, after most of the volunteers had been disbanded, Kreli having been considered as subdued. The Kafirs lost about 100 killed, while on our side only a trooper of the F.A.M.P. and one volunteer fell. Inside the earthwork were two graves, side by side, roughly railed round, with an inscription carved on a piece of wood and nailed to the stump of a tree, which ran as follows :—

SACRED
To the Memory of
H. P. BARRON,
Of the P.A.V. Guards,
and
E. WESLEY,
Of the F.A.M.P.,
Who were Killed in Action,
December 4, 1877.
Rest in Peace.

A drizzling rain set in during the night, and the morning was wet and hazy. While the column was falling in, I cantered round the Kafir positions and found several graves, in which most of the enemy's slain had been buried by the victors. I occasionally, however, encountered bones of both men and horses. We had a wet march of about twelve miles to Ibeka, where we found a large quadrangular earthwork in process of construction, to be named Fort Glyn. Large numbers of Galekas of both sexes, who had given themselves up and were living near Ibeka under the surveillance of Col. Eustace, our Resident in the Galeka country, visited the camp daily, and were supplied with rations of mealies and biltung: the women all brought from the kloofs bundles of wood for fuel, for which they received sixpence each.

The General, being about to leave for King William's Town, held a review of all the troops in the camp, which were shortly after our arrival reinforced from the colony by 100 of the volunteer force, known as "Pulleine's Rangers," under Capt. McTeggart and Lieut. Paley; also 100 of Carrington's Horse, commanded by Capt. Carrington himself: they appeared to be a fine body of men and splendidly mounted. I was informed that all the horses were selected by Capt. Carrington personally, and that several of the officers were ex-cavalry officers of the regular army.

On January 26th a column under Capt. Upcher of the 24th was ordered to march to the Quintana Mountain, and to form a camp there, together with a fort, opposite the Chichaba Valley, an extensive bush district in the Ciskei, and a favourite haunt of the Kafirs, and where they were reported to be at present in great force. This column included a detachment of the Naval Brigade under Lieut. Hamilton. Soon after its departure, a report was brought in that Gongabella's Kafirs had suffered a severe reverse in the Ciskei, and also that a large body of Gaikas had crossed into the Transkei and occupied the 'Nyameni bush, within some three miles of Upcher's camp. Three days subsequently, part of the column having marched to the outskirts of that densely wooded district, which includes all the hill country extending upwards from the left bank of the Kei, and in which are many deep valleys and rugged krantzes, had an engagement with the Kafirs, who were strongly posted: the naval force especially distinguished itself. The enemy held a high ridge, which was flanked on either side by the bush, and which was lined by a large number of Kafirs. Lieut. Hamilton, with that intrepidity for which he is well known, gallantly led his men across the Tala River; they then skirmished up the hill, although exposed to a heavy fire, which was poured into them from three sides, and as they approached the crest, suddenly forming an irregular line, charged the enemy at full speed. The Kafirs maintained a hot fire, until they had approached within thirty yards, and then, seeming astonished that the blue-jackets continued to advance, turned and fled like hares, our men occupying the position directly afterwards. Twenty dead Kafirs were counted on the ridge, and several others were probably killed in the bush. W. Peel, A.B., was severely wounded on this occasion.

Kafirs had been seen of late, spying in the vicinity of Ibeka at night, two of whom were shot by the outposts. Prisoners were sometimes brought in: one batch of twenty-five, including both Galekas and Gaikas, had been taken by Mapassa's people, having crossed at the "Ebb and Flow" drift of the Kei. One man had been badly wounded in the head. They were handcuffed and placed under a guard of Pulleine's Rangers, and as these loaded their rifles, the prisoners, although they did not move a muscle, perceptibly changed colour like chameleons, from terror, evidently expecting immediate death. The Gaikas being British subjects, and therefore rebels, were subsequently conveyed to King William's Town for trial. Our spies, the most active of whom was a female, furnished a great deal of useful information. They sometimes joined the Kafirs in the bush, and lived among them for a short period. They stated that the Gaikas, who had lately crossed the Kei, told the Galekas that in the colony they were being shot down like dogs, which seemed to intimidate them greatly.

On February 6th, several thousand Kafirs were reported to be marching on Ibeka. All the cattle which were out grazing were driven in, and every preparation made to give them a warm reception; but, later in the day, news arrived that their first attack would be directed against Capt. Upcher's' column at the Quintana Mountain. Reinforcements were at once despatched from Ibeka, consisting of some 200 Europeans, including the marines of the Naval Brigade, and detachments of the 24th regt., Carrington's Horse, Pulleine's Rangers, and of the F.A.M.P. Artillery with two seven-pounder guns, the whole under Capt. Robinson, R.A., and under my medical charge.

We set out from Ibeka, in a thick drizzle, at 4.30 p.m., and at 9 p.m. arrived at a large European-built house known as Leslie's mission station, or, in the Kafir, Tutura. This had been quite deserted for some time; all the windows had been broken, and the furniture partly destroyed, but it had not been otherwise injured. Shortly after we halted, two horsemen were despatched to inform Capt. Upcher of our arrival here. About a hundred yards from the house was a school-room, and both here and in the mission house the troops were quartered for the night. It looked very odd, when the buildings were lighted up, to see the soldiers carousing in the papered rooms, in which a good deal of the furniture remained. There was a large bell on a pole close at hand, and the marine sentry amused himself by striking the hours of the night, as if he were on board ship. Capt. Robinson and myself slept in a covered waggon, but the rain dripped through every part of the roof. The rain continued all night, and the morning was raw and foggy. I turned out about 5 a.m., and made my toilet among the wet grass, while my horse munched in a good feed of mealies beside me. I then strolled round the grounds of the mission house, which was by far the nicest place I had seen in the country. There was a neat flower-garden in front, surrounded by English shrubs, and at the side, sloping down to a stream of excellent water, was an extensive and pleasant garden, well stocked with peach, apple, fig, orange, and other fruit trees. Among these was a small rockery overrun with violets, which I was afterwards informed covered the remains of the Reverend Tyosoga, a native missionary, who was educated in Scotland and married a Scotch lady; he had several children, and resided here with Mr. Leslie. Just before 6 a.m. we heard the distant booming of guns, and a few minutes afterwards a trooper came galloping in, breathless with haste, and bearing the following note in pencil from Capt. Grenfell, one of the General's Aids-de-camp, who was with Upcher:—" Enemy is within half a mile of our camp, in force; push on at once, if possible." Forty of Pulleine's Rangers were told off as an escort of the waggons, and in a quarter of an hour the column was under way; and I do not believe that any troops could have marched better or more quickly than did the marines and the 24th on this occasion. We had about four miles to go before we could get into action—Capt. Robinson, who knew the country well, marching towards the Tala Bush, so as to make an attack on the rear of the Kafir army. I attempted to make a short cut across country, but my horse refused to jump a stream; I tried kindness, and then whip and spur, and after the animal had nearly demolished my front teeth by suddenly throwing back his head, I had to ride a circuit of fully a mile out of my way to rejoin the column. The weather still continued very thick, and I lost my road. I heard horsemen approaching, who proved to be two of the F.A.M.P. galloping towards Ibeka. I asked them the way, but all they could say was, "Don't go to the right, sir, whatever you do; there are hundreds of Kafirs there, and you'll be cut to pieces." I soon afterwards met some Fingoes, who were running away: their leader complained to me of their conduct, but I could do nothing. The fog now lifted and I saw the column, which I was not long in joining, about half a mile off. As we advanced, the rattle of rifles became incessant; a very hot fire was evidently being kept up, and occasionally there was the boom of the nine-pounder gun of the F.A.M.P. The weather now began to clear, and we saw Upcher's force on the other side of a wide ravine, pouring a brisk fire into the enemy, while Carrington's Horse was charging them at a gallop. The Kafirs were retreating, and our appearance in such a position was so unexpected that it completed their panic; we opened fire on them with shell, and they threw off their blankets to be able to run the faster. At last they all assembled on a conical hill, about two miles in advance, and, horse and foot together, there must have been at least between three and four thousand of them. Upcher's white troops were not in a position to pursue for any distance, and Robinson, whose first thought as an artilleryman was the safety of his guns, declined to attack them in their position on the hill with his force of some 140 men, and, indeed, I am not sure that such an attempt would have served any purpose, as they had only to descend the other side of the hill to enter the extensive Kei Bush, into which they all shortly disappeared. I rode across to Upcher's camp, and on the way met several bodies of Mapassa's people, who had been assisting us in the fight. I encountered Captains Upcher, Grenfell, and Carrington, who were just about to ride over the battle-field to try and count the dead, and they invited me to accompany them. The Fingoes, under Veldtman and Smith Poswa, had received orders to pursue directly that the enemy was broken, and they had commenced, according to the usual Kafir custom, by assegaing the wounded: most of the stabs were in the region of the heart. Many of the slain were old men with short grey beards, plucky old fellows evidently; here and there were horses, which also had fallen. Of the bodies which lay dead on the field, it was easy to see

at a glance which were Galekas and which Gaikas; the former looked starved, while the latter were in good condition. The warriors had all been "doctored" before the fight; they had the usual war charms round the neck, and the paint on the forehead. I took off one of these charms, consisting of two short pieces of wood fastened round the neck with a string: the wearer had evidently felt his courage flagging, for he had made two deep bites into the wood. Gneto, Kreli's witch doctor, a man of immense influence among the Galekas, was said to have sold 3000 of these charms during the week preceding this engagement, the price being about a shilling each. This action, which is known as the Battle of Quintana, from the peculiar looking hill with a solitary tree near the top, close to which it was fought, occurred as follows:—
About 5.30 a.m. the Fingo scouts came in and reported that the enemy was advancing on the camp in great force, under cover of the fog; as they came nearer they were seen to be divided into three divisions, each about 1000 strong; and the Fingoes, who occupied numerous grass huts in a valley between the enemy and the camp, were ordered to retire. All the tents were at once struck and the

The Kafir War.

troops ordered to man a quadrangular earthwork which had been thrown up to mark the site of the future fort. A company of the 24th regt., under Capt. Rainforth, was then ordered out to skirmish and retire, so as to draw the enemy onwards. The naval detachment, under Lieut. Hamilton, with a 24-pounder rocket-tube, the F.A.M.P., with a nine-pounder, and the Cape Town Artillery, with a seven-pounder gun, then opened fire. But the Kafirs still steadily advanced, even under the heavy fire from the rifles, until they came within about 400 yards; during this time many men fell, but the divisions were constantly reinforced by fresh Kafirs, who poured over the hill in the rear. After having faced a withering fire for some twenty minutes, the enemy gave way and began to retreat, and was briskly pursued by the Fingoes and Carrington's Horse. It was supposed that the Kafirs were entirely repulsed, but after some time several fresh bodies of them came out of the kloofs and advanced so boldly that one of our men was wounded by an assegai. The naval force, part of the 24th regt., and F.A.M.P., were ordered to attack them, and a determined fight ensued, which lasted for upwards of half-an-hour, when the enemy was finally repelled with heavy loss, a general retreat taking place to the conical hill I have before mentioned. The Kafirs lost between three and four hundred men in this action, while on our side only two men were killed and nine wounded; the cavalry lost several horses. The principal attacking column, and the one which fought with the greatest determination, was commanded by Gneto, the witch doctor; and both Kreli and Sandilli were said to have been present, the former being surrounded by a body-guard of 100 horsemen. Two prisoners were captured, who stated that the Kafirs made certain of taking the camp, which, from the number of tents, they judged to contain a very small body of men: their plans were to kill every one, plunder the waggons, attack Mapassa's people, and then to march on Ibeka. Upcher's force consisted of 436 white troops and 560 Fingoes.

On the succeeding day our whole force advanced on the 'Nyameni and the Tala Bush, where the defeated enemy was supposed to be taking refuge. In front of us was the conical hill on which the Kafirs had assembled after their overthrow; and a troop of our cavalry, under Capt. Von Courtland, was sent forward to examine it, as it was thought that a large body of the enemy was probably awaiting us behind its brow. It was a matter of great interest to watch the horsemen slowly ascend in a gradually narrowing semicircle, until they formed a compact body on the summit, when we expected to see several saddles emptied; but, to our relief, the men waved their hats to inform us that the farther side of the hill was quite clear of Kafirs, after which we immediately occupied it. While the cavalry was ascending I was much amused at a remark of one of our blue-jackets:—A volunteer kindly offered him a drink of rum from his flask; he rejected it in the most indignant manner, and interlarding his answer with several by no means polished adjectives, he remarked that "he wasn't going to have any blessed Dutch Courage." From this point we saw below and on our right the dense Tala Bush, beyond that and also in front of us the Kei, and on the further side of that river the thickly-wooded Chichaba Valley; on our left were several deep and rugged ravines full of trees; indeed, the entire locality was one vast bush. Our force occupied all the commanding points, on which the guns and rockets were placed, and the Fingoes went through several parts of the bush. In a short time we saw numerous Kafirs "treking" away, but quite beyond the range of our guns, and the number of intervening kloofs effectually prevented any pursuit. Far away, on our right, a white speck was visible, which by the aid of a field-glass was seen to be the camp at " the springs," held by a volunteer force; and we hoped that they would observe the Kafirs coming in their direction, and advance to the attack; but in this we were disappointed, and the enemy having assembled for a short time on a distant hill, as if engaged in a consultation, gradually dissolved from view as only Kafirs can. As our Fingoes advanced through the bush we kept up a steady fire across the kloofs with shells and rockets, and I am much afraid that both women and children suffered on this occasion through foolishly remaining in the bush; and the Fingoes, seeing red blankets moving about, of course fired. They collected a body of about fifteen women and twenty children, and brought them into the open. Capt. Morshead, of the 24th, and myself rode down to the spot with an interpreter to question them as to the situation of the Kafir army. Some of the women looked wretchedly ill: one had been slightly wounded in the knee by a bullet, which afterwards lodged deeply in the thigh of the little child she was carrying. I extracted the ball with some little difficulty, and all the women were loud in their exclamations of astonishment as I drew out the large flattened piece of lead. The mother seemed very fond of her child, and expressed her gratitude. I told her that, if she would come to my tent in two days' time, I would attend further to the wound; upon which a very intelligent-looking female remarked that "they were never afraid to go to a white man's camp, it was the Fingoes they dreaded," and against them they seemed to be very bitter. Another woman held a newly-born baby in her arms. To one or two who looked very exhausted I gave some brandy from my flask, but, there being no water to mix with it, it burnt their throats, made them cough desperately, and their tears flow. They said something about "devil's water" and "sorcery," and were evidently suspicious of us, so to undeceive them I drank a small quantity myself, but, as it affected me in much the same manner that it did them, it occasioned peals of laughter. The Galekas were not accustomed to drink anything stronger than their weak native beer, for Kreli would never allow any spirits to be brought into his territory. There was a certain amount of good breeding about some of these females. One of them, a young woman, had a very nice bag made of wild cat skin which I requested. She handed it to me, but very reluctantly, and I could perceive how sorry she was to part with it; upon which I returned it. Her face beamed with pleasure, and she received it with a bow which would have done credit to an English lady at a drawing-room, but immediately spoiled the effect by lighting up a very dirty pipe and beginning to spit. As there were no Kafirs to be found, we returned to camp in the afternoon, but subsequently made a second search, on a different plan.

The cavalry on this occasion started at 3.30 a.m., while it was yet dark, and occupied the heights to the eastward of the Tala Valley. When they had proceeded for a short distance, they found the ground strewed with cooking utensils, female ornaments, mats, &c. One officer picked up a small tortoise made into a purse, and containing twenty-five shillings. Late last evening, as one of our waggons from Ibeka, laden with ammunition, had arrived within a mile of the camp, under a strong guard of Fingoes, brisk firing was heard, and as it was supposed that Kafirs were attacking it, Inspector Springer, with twenty of the F.A.M.P., was ordered to ride with all speed and reinforce the guard. On his arrival he found the Fingoes firing into the darkness, but none of the enemy were returning it. It was evident that a large body of Kafirs, principally females, passing from one part of the country to another, were spending the night at this spot; and the Fingoes, seeing fires smouldering in the darkness close by them, and hearing the Kafir language, thought they were about to be attacked; and their noise, added to that of Springer's men dashing up the hill, made the Kafirs suppose that they were being surrounded, and they fled precipitately, leaving all their valuables behind them. A strong column of artillery and infantry, including the naval detachment, with several hundred Fingoes under Commandant Pattle, left the camp at 4.30 a.m. and searched the country to the west of the Tala Bush, as well as the bush itself, the troops at "the springs" also co-operating; but the enemy had left the neighbourhood, as only a few cattle were captured and half-a-dozen kraals burned. The little Galeka child from whom

I extracted the bullet was brought to my tent by its mother, so that I might dress the wound. During the operation the lady sat on a box in my tent and smoked her pipe; but as politeness forbade her spitting on the floor, she very considerately used a fold of the red blanket she wore. We afterwards struck our tents, to return to Ibeka; whilst this was being done, a number of Mapassa's people came into the camp to see what they could pick up. They were very badly off for food, and seized with avidity the mealies which the horses had left. One woman spoke intensely grammatical English; she seemed a respectable female, and had several children with her. She informed me that she belonged to Anta's people, in the Ciskei, but that she had married a Galeka; that she had been educated at the seminary at Lovedale, that Mapassa's people were starving, and she longed for the war to be over, for she was quite certain that, as the Xosa were beaten in every engagement, they must succumb in the end, and that their continuing to fight was madness. All the family were very thin, and one of the daughters pinched up the skin over her stomach to signify how empty she was; so I procured a lot of spare biscuit and gave the mother, which she at once distributed.

Soon after our return to Ibeka we buried A. Mabey, a drummer of the Royal Marines, who died of dysentery: he was interred in a valley to the west of the camp, beneath three large trees.

The next march of the Naval Brigade was to our old neighbourhood, the western side of the Quora Bush, in which extensive thickets Kreli was reported to lie with the bulk of his army, having collected them there after his reverse at Quintana. On this occasion we took with us a twelve-pounder Armstrong, drawn by a span of bullocks. The strength of our column was 2325, the 325 being European troops. The naval detachment was commanded by Lieut. Hamilton, and the whole was under the command of Capt. Upcher. Col. Glyn also left with another column for the eastern part of the Quora Bush, and with this force we were to act in concert. We had a very pleasant march; as the preceding days had been wet, there was no dust, and everything was deliciously green. We gathered large quantities of mushrooms on the road, which were very acceptable additions to our diet. Just after passing Luzesi, detachments crossed the Quora at different points and burned large numbers of kraals, besides killing several Kafirs, the remainder flying to the bush on horseback. On the march I met with many skulls and other relics of those who had been slain during the past few months. On the third evening of our advance, a portion of our force had a warm engagement with a large body of Kafirs which held the outskirts of the Quora Bush. We had two men killed and one wounded. We captured 95 head of cattle, and the loss of the enemy in men was probably heavy, as our fire was well maintained; but as they dragged most of their killed and wounded into the bush, and darkness came on, it is impossible to estimate their loss. One or two of the bodies which we found were evidently those of Gaikas, as they had Government passes on them; similar passes were also discovered on several bodies after the fight at Quintana. This skirmish was perhaps unfortunate, as on the following day, when we made a complete search through the bush and shelled all the neighbouring kloofs with our Armstrong gun, not a Kafir was to be found; they had evidently all withdrawn during the night.

The Kafir War. 151

Part of our force now joined Col. Glyn's column; the other part, including the Naval Brigade, returned to Ibeka, and we marched that distance, about twenty-four miles, in one day, giving the bullocks an outspan of two hours on the road. The weather was cool and the ground in good condition after the recent rains. As we arrived opposite the Gaudana Mountain, the horizon began to get hazy, and a slight downpour commenced with a sound of distant thunder; then the sky around us suddenly got black and a terrific thunderstorm ensued; the long brilliant forks of lightning seemed to strike the ground all around us, followed instantaneously by the deafening crash of thunder. The rain descended in sheets, the grass-land becoming speedily converted into a lake, while torrents, like small rivers, swept the waggon-track; both our horses and ourselves held down our heads to escape the beating of the rain. Our blue-jackets marched ahead in a double line, up to their knees in water, followed closely by Hamilton and myself on horseback. They sang a song nearly the whole time, called "The Turkey and the Bear," which I supposed to have some allusion to European affairs; and whenever the thunder pealed with unusual violence, so their song became additionally loud. Although saturated with rain, they seemed to consider the whole thing as particularly enjoyable.

Three days after our arrival at Ibeka, I again set out to take medical charge of Col. Glyn's column, then encamped at Willowdale, about twenty-five miles distant, and to which our marines belonged. I left Ibeka with an escort of Carrington's Light Horse, several waggons laden with stores accompanying me, in charge of an officer of the commissariat. We outspanned at a deserted store known as "Barnet's shop," the late proprietor of which now kept the store at Ibeka; here we were joined by a body of Fingoes, which had been ordered to assemble there, to act as a guard to the waggons. Just beyond this place there was a nasty drift to cross, the banks of the river were very steep, and the stream was much swollen by the heavy rains; the mud was dreadful, and, to complete our discomfiture, a heavy thunderstorm came on. Some of the waggons crossed, but the heavier ones stuck fast in mid-stream, and we had to put on additional spans of oxen; sometimes there were as many as fifty-two

The Kafir War. 153

pulling at one waggon before it could be extricated. The men of Carrington's Horse, consisting principally of colonial farmers, dismounted and superintended, and the cracking of whips, the shouting and yelling to get them to pull together, were beyond description; sometimes an ox would lie down from pure stubbornness, when he had about six men flogging at him until he got up again. We were altogether about three hours crossing this drift, during which time I sat on horseback, with my back to the rain, giving directions, while the commissariat officer looked after the waggons which had crossed. The roads were very heavy as we proceeded; it began to get dark, and as there was no chance of reaching Col. Glyn's camp that night, I was just on the point of giving directions to bivouac, when I descried a small collection of white tents about a mile in advance. I pushed on and found that it was a small camp of the 24th regt., under Lieut. Heaton. He informed me that Col. Glyn's camp was some six miles further, so I sent on six Fingoes with some despatches I carried, and outspanned for the night, Lieut. Heaton kindly giving me some supper and part of his tent. The next morning we received intelligence that Glyn's column was approaching, and that we were to encamp about two miles further on, where it would join us. It is a good rule in campaigning, whenever it can be done, to make a full meal in the early morning, as an old officer remarked, "I always start early, but I never start empty; I always march on a beef-steak and hot coffee," and I acted on this advice to-day. When we had arrived near the appointed place, and the tents were being pitched, the commissariat officer and myself walked up to the top of a low rocky ridge, about five hundred yards distant from the camp, to see what was behind it, as Kafirs might easily have found shelter there for firing amongst the tents. On our arrival we saw some vegetable marrows growing about a couple of hundred yards below, close to where a kraal had been formerly burned, and we walked down to procure some. We had not been there long when two Kafirs arrived, both armed with assegais. My companion asked them, in the Kafir language, where they were going: they answered, "Oh, only looking about!" I suggested that we should make them prisoners, but my companion thought they might be Fingoes; so I borrowed his revolver, as I had no arms with me, and requested that he would return to the camp and ask Lieut. Heaton to send down some Fingoes to ascertain who they were. In the meantime I stood sentry over them within easy pistol-shot, so as to be ready if they attempted to attack me with their assegais. They eyed the revolver, and then slowly wandered back down the kloof. I did not care to follow, as I could not tell what number there might not be in the bush. In about ten minutes a body of Fingoes, with guns and assegais, and one of Carrington's Horse, with his rifle, came running down the hill. We crept towards the bush and surrounded them, the Fingoes at once saying that they were Kafirs. The men said that they were, but that they possessed passes, which they were told to produce: they both turned out their bags, which were full of green stuff, but there was no pass: their assegais were then taken away and they were conveyed to the camp. Col. Glyn, who had by this time arrived, ordered that they should be examined. They now said that they belonged to a Government reserve, upon which their assegais were returned, and they were allowed to depart. It is extremely likely that these men were fighting Kafirs, who were "treking" about in small bodies in search of food, according to their custom, as they possessed no passes and were far outside the boundary of any reserve. The strength of our column was 546 European troops and 2600 Fingoes. The next evening, after a very hot day's march, we encamped at Malan's mission station. An officer's rifle-match here took place among the crack shots of the different corps. After some remarkably good shooting, the prize was taken by an officer of the Naval Brigade, Lieut. Dowding, who commanded the marines. Our column was here broken up and divided into three parts, one to remain in the present camp, under the command of Capt. Harrison of the 24th, one to march to and encamp at Beecham Wood, near the sea, about twenty miles further off, and one to occupy Barnet's shop; thus the four posts of Ibeka, Barnet's shop, Malan's mission, and Beecham Wood formed a chain across the country and prevented the return of any Galekas who had been driven across the Bashee. The camp at Malan's, where I remained, was at no great distance from the 'Mbongo Mountain, and, as the crow flies, not more than ten or twelve miles from the

The Kafir War.

Bashee, and we often observed what were evidently signal-fires burning on the hill-tops in the Bomvana country. A quadrangular earthwork was being thrown up here under the direction of Lieut. Main, R.E., also a similar one at Beecham Wood. Parties of Fingoes went out daily to reconnoitre and try to find the hiding-place of Kreli, which discovery had not yet been made, notwithstanding that a thousand pounds had long been offered for his capture. He was supposed never to have left his country, but to be still concealed in some part of the vast Quora Bush, with two or three attendants. Great precautions seem to have been taken with regard to his seclusion. It was said that when a Kafir brought him provisions he knew somewhere about the locality in which he was secreted, and called out that he had food for the chief; then one of the personal attendants approached by a circuitous route, and, having climbed a tree, called out that he was coming; he then made another round, until he reached the man and took the food; but this only made " assurance doubly sure," as the Kafirs are most loyal to their great chiefs, and there was little chance of his being betrayed by his people.

After remaining here a few days we received orders to return to Ibeka *en route* for East London, and there to embark in H.M. troopship "Himalaya" for conveyance to the "Active" at Simon's Town. The marines having arrived from Beecham Wood, we set out on our return, and, after a very tiresome march of fifteen miles, we outspanned close to the stream, near Barnet's shop, to which place I strolled up and visited the officers of Carrington's Horse, who were quartered there, the men having extemporized all kinds of huts and shelters close round it. The Kafirs seemed to have occupied it at one time, probably before the action at Gandana, as a fire had been lighted in the middle of the room after their fashion in a hut, which had burned a large circular hole in the boarded floor; and they had, besides, fired numerous bullets through the corrugated iron sides of the building out of pure devilry. Beyond this place we killed a night adder, and a snake known as a ringhaltz, a most venomous-looking reptile, about six feet long and nearly as thick as one's arm. When we approached within three miles of Ibeka we saw some horsemen approaching, who proved to be Hamilton and Cochran of the Naval Brigade, and Thirkill of the 88th, who had ridden out to meet us; some distance further on we met Major Logan of the 24th, and behind him the drums and fifes of that regiment, which had come out to play us into camp. That evening we all dined together in Lieut. Hamilton's tent, and the band of the 24th played in the Naval Brigade camp. The next day, March 10th, our tents were struck, our waggons loaded, and our men under arms by 6 a.m., Col. Glyn, Major Logan, Lieutenants Hodson, Clements, and Cavage of the 24th, and many other of our friends, being present to wish us "good-bye," Lieut. Thirkill of the 88th riding with us as far as Butterworth, and the drum-and-fife band of the 24th heading us for above a mile. We passed through Butterworth just as the Fingo congregation was coming out of Mr. Warner's church, the Sunday attire of the women being composed of the most gorgeous colours. I saw one of our blue-jackets, who was leading a monkey by a string, stealthily creep up behind a body of them; and when they looked round and saw what they regard as an "uncanny" animal, and about which they are very superstitious, close at their heels, they gave several shrieks, and ran in all directions, to the sailor's intense delight. We had with us three Kafir prisoners of some notoriety, and the guard had orders to shoot them should they attempt to escape; they were all Gaikas, and one of them had been taken when spying near our camp at Quintana and had been shot in the head. The rain commenced as we left Butterworth, and we came to a difficult drift, which greatly delayed us. We did not see the lights of Tolene till after midnight, and as, from the hilly nature of the country and the exhausted state of our oxen, we could not reach it, we outspanned about a mile off, close to a large Fingo kraal. A tolerably good road extended from Tolene to the Kei. The country was everywhere of an emerald hue, dotted by what looked like circles of mushrooms, but which really were Fingo kraals, while large numbers of cattle grazed among the valleys.

Our next outspan was near the Kei drift, where we were joined by Lieut. Craigie of the Naval Brigade, and Mr. Yates, interpreter, who had ridden from Komgha to meet us, and very glad we were to see them again. We afterwards crossed the Kei drift, the water just coming up to the noses of the oxen. We were very fortunate, as it was the only day for upwards of a fortnight that the Kei had been fordable, and it was again rising. One waggon, that had tried to cross in the early morning laden with wool, had stuck in the drift, and was probably washed away during the night. Our men crossed by the bridge, and the guard took especial precautions to prevent the prisoners escaping while passing through the bush country, on the colonial side of the Kei: a blue-jacket had passed a noose round the neck of the principal prisoner, and tied the other end round his own waist, so that should he attempt an escape he would strangle himself: this Kafir had also a circle of feathers stuck upright around his head, which gave him a somewhat imposing appearance, and every one that passed us supposed he was Kreli. Having crossed the river, as the waggons could not start for some time, I rode on with Craigie and Yates. The road from this to Pullen's farm was about five miles in length, and wound up to the high lands through numerous kloofs, everywhere filled with dense bush. When we had proceeded a short distance, and it was getting dark, a heavy thunderstorm came on; the rain was tremendous, and the darkness was increased by the thick overhanging bush, except when momentarily illuminated by the lightning, which was so exceedingly bright that occasionally we became temporarily blinded; the crash of the thunder was re-echoed through the kloofs, and the drenching rain soon rendered the roads very muddy and slippery. A waggon had outspanned by the road-side, and fourteen of the oxen were killed in a moment by the lightning. In a former war the Kafirs caused much destruction in this neighbourhood by waylaying and attacking convoys, and a few days before some fourteen Kafirs had been killed here who were lying concealed with a similar object. As we came near an unusually deep and dark kloof, Craigie would remark, " If there happen to be any Kafirs here to-night, we shall be assegaied before we know where we are." We felt our way, so to speak, down the kloof, and, directly our horses' hoofs touched the bottom, we spurred them into a gallop and dashed up the hill, so as to escape any assegais which might be thrown; but I imagine that the weather was too wet for Kafirs to be abroad. As we got towards the top, the lightning became of a brilliant red colour, and the thunder occasionally made a noise like the discharge of a rocket, as if a thunderbolt were whizzing through the air. My horse came down in the slippery road and temporarily lamed himself, so that I could get him no farther than Pullen's farm, where Lieut. Moore, with his detachment of the 88th, still remained, and he was good enough to give me a rug on the ground.

On my arrival the next morning at Komgha, I found Capt. Wright, Mr. Marwood, Lieut. Craigie, and Sub-Lieut. Barnes-Lawrence, and in the tent of the two latter I had the only civilized meal I had eaten for three months; they appeared to be very popular at Komgha, and on one occasion had given a ball in the school-house, which had been a great success. I was here also most hospitably entertained by Dr. Macartney, of the army medical department, an officer who had seen much service against the Gaikas in the neighbourhood. Having here joined the Ciskei division of the Naval Brigade, we all marched direct to the Kei Road railway station, which we hoped to reach in a couple of days. On our way we passed the charred remains of the hotel at Dribosch. The only living thing about the place was a fine peacock, which had somehow escaped the pillage:

one of our men took possession of it, for conveyance to the ship. Further on we came to Fort Wellington, where there was an encampment of the Diamond Field Horse, under Col. Warren, R.E. The officers were very kind, and entertained us at luncheon. Poor fellows! two of them very shortly afterwards fell in action at the Peri Bush. When we arrived at Kei Road, Wright, Dowding, Barnes-Lawrence, and the marines, were suddenly ordered to King William's Town, to join the troops under General Thesiger, who had superseded Sir A. Cunynghame, which were about to attack the Peri Bush; they were afterwards reinforced by thirty bluejackets with rockets, under Lieut. Craigie. The remainder of the brigade took the train to Panmure. On our road we found all the goods sheds and railway stores filled with refugees from the surrounding country. On our arrival at that place we could see the "Himalaya" lying off East London, waiting for us to embark. We went on board her the next day, March 16th, having been landed exactly three months, and on the evening of the 18th we arrived at Simon's Bay. The commodore came off to receive us directly that we had anchored, which he did most cor-

The Kafir War.

dially, and the same evening we rejoined the "Active."

About three weeks subsequently a steamer arrived in Simon's Bay with the remainder of the Naval Brigade, which had been detached for service against the Gaikas in the neighbourhood of King William's Town, and we were glad to find that it returned without any losses.

I have already mentioned that a few days after the Naval Brigade landed in British Kaffraria, Lieut. Craigie, Sub-Lieut. Barnes-Lawrence, Mr. Bays, gunner, and 100 men, with two guns, were ordered to march to Fort Cunynghame, in the Ciskei, and garrison that place. They arrived there on December 20th, after a hot and weary march, relieving a detachment of the 88th regt. Lieut. Craigie was the commandant of this fort, which was a square stone building at the foot of the Amatola Mountains, on the border of the Gaika location, about six miles from Stutterheim, and it commanded the main road from King William's Town to Queenstown. A chain, comprising three fortresses, extended along this road, the other two being Forts Cathcart and Tylden. About eighteen miles from Fort Cunynghame, on the Kabousie

River, which is a tributary of the Kei, was one of the kraals of Sandilli, the great Gaika chief. A day or two before our detachment took up its quarters in the fort, Kiva, a Galeka chief, with a following from his tribe, had crossed the Kei. On Craigie's arrival, he remarked that all the neighbouring kraals were tenanted by women and children only, the men having gone to Kabousie to attend a tribal meeting at Sandilli's kraal. He likewise started to attend this assembly, accompanied by Mr. Wright, the resident magistrate, and, on nearing the kraal, observed about 250 men, clothed in the usual red blanket, all armed with assegais, and about one third carrying guns. These were mostly percussion muskets: some had flint locks, some were fowling-pieces, and there were a few rifles. About a tenth of the men were mounted. On arriving at the kraal, they perceived about seventy men seated beneath a tree. Sandilli advanced to meet his visitors; he appeared to be an elderly man, about six feet two inches in height, well proportioned, with a Roman nose, and lame in one leg. He drew them to one side, and after they had been joined by one of his, Sandilli's, sons and three chiefs, Mr. Wright told Sandilli that their object in coming was because they "had heard that Kiva was in his location, and they desired to know what he had come for."

Sandilli: "How did you hear?"

Mr. Wright: "By letter from King William's Town."

Sandilli: "Why did you come? did you think I would not tell you of it?"

Mr. Wright: "It was necessary to come directly I heard of it, to prevent any trouble arising."

Sandilli: "Kiva is here; I have sent for him to know what he is doing: when I get the word of the tribe respecting him, I will come and tell you. The assembly here to-day says that the matter should be referred to Tyala, Soga, Finn, and Kona, and I have sent messengers to these chiefs; when I get their reply I will let you know; I wish Government to take no steps against Kiva till I get their reply."

Mr. Wright: "There is great danger in delay: Kiva has come from the war, and is the Queen's enemy: armed parties might be in search, and might come into collision with the Gaikas: your people should be warned not to interfere with any party in pursuit of Kiva."

Sandilli: "Gaikas will not interfere with those parties, but I wish the Government to wait till the tribe has given its verdict about Kiva."

Mr. Wright: "How long will that be?"

Sandilli: "I cannot hear until the day after to-morrow."

Mr. Wright: "Why do all your people come armed?"

Sandilli: "It is the usual thing; we learn these things from Government, which is constantly drilling its men under arms. Why does Government treat me like this, when I am taking the part of a neutral in this war? why, when refugees come to me, does not the Government demand them, instead of sending in pursuit?"

Mr. Wright: "Government holds the right of pursuing its enemies even among independent tribes, much more so among the Gaikas, who are subjects. When Kreli fled, he was pursued among the Bomvanas and Pondos, none questioning the matter of right."

The interview then terminated. The total number of armed Gaikas about Sandilli's kraal on this occasion may be estimated at 600, and their demeanour was sullen, and even threatening. On the following day the war-cry was heard about Fort Cunynghame, and bodies of men were seen assembling at the kraals of the local chiefs from all quarters.

A few days later, Lieut. Craigie and Mr. Wright had another interview with Sandilli, at his more distant kraal of Kemimi, near the Kei, in the northern part of the Gaika location; on this occasion they were accompanied by twenty-five troopers of the F.A.M.P. While there the war-cry was sounded, and bodies of armed Gaikas were seen hurrying towards the Kei, as it was rumoured that the Fingoes had fired across the river. Craigie requested Sandilli to stop them, which he did, and called several of them back. Considerable confusion ensued, and, when order was restored, they requested to be informed what had been done regarding Kiva. Tyala, one of the old chiefs present, replied thus :—"The Gaika tribe is here to-day to give its word: Kiva is to return from whence he came; messengers are to go at once with the word of the tribe to that effect." Sandilli then remarked, "I am sincere in saying that I wish to sit still. The Fingoes have crossed the Kei and have seized cattle; the Gaikas turned out in pursuit, recaptured the cattle and burned some kraals; I wish the Government to keep the Fingoes quiet." Mr. Wright here explained the duties of the Gaikas, as British subjects, in the matter of Kiva, according to the terms of his instructions received from the Government. Three reports of the seizure of cattle—whether genuine ones is questionable—were made to Sandilli in their presence, and he detailed parties to restore the cattle to their owners. Messengers were also depatched to Kiva, ordering him to move at once, and that no reply was necessary. There were about 1000 armed Gaikas at this meeting; such an assemblage looked very menacing, considering the aspect of affairs at such a time, but its bearing appeared more friendly than at the Kabousie Conference. On the return of Lieut. Craigie to Fort Cunynghame, he received a report that Gaikas had seized Fingo stock the evening before, and shot one of the drivers, and that very morning, also, cattle were seized and Fingo huts burned. On this very day, also, the Gaikas vigorously attacked the F.A.M.P. under Major Moore of the 88th, near Dribosch, and shortly afterwards a detachment of the 88th was assailed in the same neighbourhood.

As it was evident that the rebellion had

actually broken out, a proclamation was issued that all Gaikas who wished to be loyal and not to fight against the Government should come and be registered; and on January 11th, a meeting of the so-called loyal Gaikas was convened at Fort Cunynghame for the purpose of ascertaining how many men actually in that neighbourhood had registered. There were present 782 men, with 203 guns and 1800 assegais, and the total number registered was found to be 1418 men, with 223 guns, 3500 assegais, and 10,500 head of cattle. The men registered were provided with "passes." During this muster all the blue-jackets were kept under arms in case of treachery, but the affair passed off very quietly. Advantage was taken of this occasion to exhibit some shell practice to the Kafirs, which seemed to impress them greatly. Both Craigie and Barnes-Lawrence did great service while here in disarming these so-called loyal Gaikas, in which process they frequently incurred great personal risks. Towards the end of January the naval detachment was relieved by the Port Elizabeth Militia, and marched to Komgha, with the exception of Mr. Bays, gunner, who proceeded to King William's Town in command of a small body of men, with two guns.

It was afterwards actively engaged as part of a column of troops in scouring the formidable Chichaba Valley. The Naval Brigade indeed seems to have been ubiquitous: it had simultaneously detachments at Komgha, Ibeka, in the field, in the Transkei, Fort Cunynghame, and King William's Town, and artillery with each detachment; and latterly, at the Peri Bush, where its conduct was highly spoken of by the General, and where the rockets in particular, under Sub-Lieut. Barnes-Lawrence, did much execution.

THE ZULU WAR.

THE

NAVAL BRIGADE IN ZULULAND, 1879.

BEFORE commencing an account of the operations of the Naval Brigade against the Zulus, it will perhaps be interesting to give a brief history of that nation, and of the state of affairs which conduced to bring about the war.

The Zulus date themselves as a nation from the time of Chaka, or Tjaka, which name signifies "a fury," fifty or sixty years ago. He it was who conquered all the surrounding tribes, and converted their kings into his chiefs, or Indunas. His territory is said to have extended from the Pondo country to Delagoa Bay, and inland it included part of the Transvaal and Orange Free State. The Zulus, from the earliest traditions, were a small tribe, which, coming from the northwest, wandered about until it settled down peaceably in the district now known as Amahlabatini; hence its name, signifying "a vagabond." Before the time of Chaka they were immediately ruled by his father, Usenzangakoni, who married Umnande, a daughter of Dingiswayo, the king of the Umtetwa people, who inhabited a part of the present Zulu country, and who was also paramount chief of the comparatively small Zulu tribe. The reigning Zulu chieftains, for their subsequent security, always made it a custom to slay their male children; but Umnande, just before giving birth to Chaka, visited her father, at whose kraal she left her child, under the guardianship of Umgumani, one of his principal Indunas, and so preserved his life. Neither Chaka nor the Zulus ever forgot this act of maternal solicitude, and at Umnande's death a long period of general mourning was ordered, during which large numbers of people, to show the extent of their grief for the departed, slew themselves, and, in their usual metaphorical manner, destroyed large numbers of cows which possessed young calves, so that the latter might starve to death, and thus, in company with the nation, feel how terrible it is to be bereaved of a mother. It was Dingiswayo who first raised the Zulu regiments and incorporated them in a standing army. He is reported to have copied his system from the white troops in the west; and as no women were seen with these, he concluded that they were not allowed to marry, and framed his new military laws accordingly.

On the death of Usenzangakoni, Dingiswayo appointed his grandson Chaka to succeed him. This monarch greatly developed the military system already introduced; how he subjugated all the neighbouring tribes I have already mentioned; and at the head of these he placed the Zulus, and would allow no other language than theirs to be spoken in his presence. The Zulu nation of to-day thus consists of numerous tribes, each presided over by its particular chief; every one has its patronymic, of which it is exceedingly proud; and whenever one man speaks with another belonging to a different tribe, it is always considered the etiquette to address him by the name of that tribe. There is not a boy who cannot tell his tribal patronymic. The ruling idea of Chaka was that he would reign supreme over all the black races, and he was willing that the English should in like manner govern the white—a sentiment which has been jealously perpetuated by his successors. Although Chaka ruled his people with unmitigated severity, every Zulu speaks of him with pride, especially with reference to his military prowess. Besides amending or modifying many of their customs—and, among other things, he abolished the practice of circumcision—he also introduced a very important military reform; for whereas, before his time, the Zulus employed their assegais as missiles, Chaka insisted on their using a short or stabbing assegai, so as to bring them into close quarters with their enemies. This king was assassinated by his brother Dingaan at Stanger, in Natal, towards the latter part of 1828.

Dingaan then became king. His reign was marked by every species of bloodshed and cruelty; he murdered all his brothers excepting Umpanda, or Panda, and he spared him probably on account of his peaceable disposition, and because he had refused, when requested, to be made king. His treacherous slaughter of Retief and his Boers is well known: from 90 to 100 Boers had visited him with the object of entering into a treaty; they were hospitably received, the king acceded to their demands, and, as they were preparing to return home, he invited them to an entertainment at his kraal. They were told that they must leave their arms outside, as it was contrary to etiquette to take them in; they were then immediately set upon and butchered, only one or two escaping. The incensed Boers invaded Zululand; but their army was destroyed by having been treacherously led into a kloof called Lupati, in the Umslatoosi Bush, where the Zulus were lying in ambush, by a man called Bongoza. Panda at length revolted, and, having joined the Boers under Pretorius, the Zulu country was again invaded. Dingaan's army was routed, but he himself escaped and fled to the Swazis, who put him to death. This happened in 1840. Panda was now invested with the sovereignty by the Boers. His reign, compared with those of his predecessors, was clement; and, contrary to their custom, he spared the lives of his children. The Rev. Mr. Robertson, who was intimately acquainted with this king, informed me that he was much troubled about the nomination of a successor; that he was very averse to Ketchwayo becoming ruler of the Zulus; and that he favoured his son Umbulazi. There was much difference of opinion in the country, until at length a serious civil war ensued, the opposite factions being headed by the two brothers. The rival armies met near the left bank of the Tugela, in December, 1856, and, after a severe struggle, Umbulazi was defeated with great loss, and he himself slain. Fearful atrocities were perpetrated in this engagement; many hundreds of men, women, and children, who sought safety by endeavouring to cross into Natal, were attacked while in the River Tugela and butchered: the broad stream was red with blood, and the shores of Natal were strewed with the bodies which had been cast up by the sea. It was in this action that Mr. John Dunn first came into notice. Having crossed the Tugela, with a body of men carrying fire-arms, he joined Umbulazi, and caused much loss to the enemy. When his army was defeated, he courageously covered the retreat, being eventually obliged to leap his horse into the Tugela, where many of his men perished, and he himself narrowly escaped.

In 1861, the Government of Natal induced Panda to name Ketchwayo his successor. Panda died a natural death in October, 1872, after reigning some two-and-thirty years. As the great Chaka had always acknowledged

the supremacy of the English, and with the hope that we should subsequently support his authority against any rival who might arise, some few months after Panda's death a request arrived from Ketchwayo that the Government of Natal would send a representative to instal him as king of the Zulu nation. Consequently, in August 1873, Mr. (now Sir) T. Shepstone, known among the Zulus as "Somtseu," with an escort of 110 Natal Volunteers, journeyed to the Amahlabatini and installed Ketchwayo as king, in the presence of his relatives, Indunas, and an immense concourse of the Zulu people, and that without those horrible scenes of bloodshed which had usually marked the accession of the Zulu monarchs. On this occasion the following important Articles were arranged:—
"That the amicable relations existing in the time of Panda between the Zulus and Natal Government should continue, and should be strengthened if possible; that the indiscriminate shedding of blood should cease; that for minor offences fines should be instituted; that no Zulu should be condemned to death without a fair public trial; that he should have the right of appeal to the king; and that after this process his life should not

be taken without the king's order. In cases of alleged witchcraft, the crime for which the punishment of death was most frequently inflicted, that the conduct of the accused should be further tested before he was condemned." These were important concessions on the part of the king and his councillors, and must have been very grateful to the people. Mr. Shepstone also attempted to bring about the abolition of witch doctors; yet the belief in witchcraft was so strong that the people thought that, if these impostors were suppressed, the wizards and witches would become so powerful that fearful destruction would ensue, so that nothing decisive could be achieved. Neither Ketchwayo nor his great predecessor Chaka seem themselves to have had any real faith in these men.

Ketchwayo laboured hard to foster the military spirit, and to develope yet further the regimental system promoted by his uncle Chaka: his army was powerful, and, for a savage race, highly disciplined; it was divided into several corps, some including several regiments, as the Undi corps. Every regiment had its particular name: for example, the Nokenke, meaning "the dividers;" Umhlanga, "a bed of reeds;" Umcityu,

Umbonambi, Tulwana, &c.: it had also its distinctive uniform or badge, such as a band of leopard or other skin around the head, ear-flaps of certain skins, coloured spots on the shields, or particular feathers on the head. Every male in the Zulu country, from the ages of about sixteen to seventy, being a soldier, was not allowed to marry without the king's special permission, and this was granted to a whole regiment at a time, and generally not before the men had reached some forty years of age. There were thus married regiments and unmarried regiments; the former were known by the ring of black resin round the head, and by their using a white shield; the unmarried men wore no ring, and their shields were black. When the war broke out, there were in all about thirty-three regiments and corps—nineteen married and fourteen unmarried; they differed greatly as to numerical strength, for, as a corps got old, so it snumbers diminished, for the vacancies were not filled; thus one regiment might be two or three thousand strong, another only perhaps as many hundreds. Before the commencement of the war, a Zulu army list was published, which placed the numbers of the entire force at

40,400, but this was far below the real fighting strength. A gentleman of my acquaintance, who was once present at Ulundi when the army had been called up by the king, counted the number of companies present, and he estimated the strength of the army at from 65,000 to 70,000. I made inquiries of those most familiar with the Zulu army as to how many fire-arms it possessed at the commencement of the war. The mean of four opinions gave about 9000; but as the number supplied by way of Delagoa Bay seemed very uncertain, 10,000 may probably be regarded as a close approximation to the reality. The men who carried fire-arms bore no shields as a rule, but every one was provided with short or stabbing assegais, and many also with a "knobkerry," which was used something in the same manner as an old knight wielded his mace. The shields were of an oval shape, made of bullock's hide slashed down the centre, and behind them was a long vertical stick surmounted by the tail of a wild cat. These regiments had numerous large military kraals about the country, some of them containing several hundred huts, and at these the men of each district assembled when the king gave the order for the regiments to be embodied, after which they usually were "massed" at Ulundi. When collected together, feuds often arose among the regiments, fights would ensue, and much bloodshed was the consequence; this especially took place when married and unmarried regiments were quartered near each other. The Zulu order of battle and method of attack date from the days of Chaka, and perhaps were in vogue before his time. The attacking force consists of a dense body of men, the foremost forming the chest, the hindermost the loins of the army, and from the sides of these two long bodies are thrown out called the horns; these extend themselves with great rapidity, so as to try and completely encircle the enemy. Behind them is posted a large reserve, which is kept under arms, with its back turned towards the fight. Before the army engages, the General directs an Umkumbu, or semicircle, to be formed, when he delivers his orders; after this he takes up a position on some commanding height, with a staff of runners, who act as his aides-de-camp and convey his instructions to the engaged regiments: with the General a second and smaller reserve is usually posted. A Zulu army, when on the march, always appears to be much larger than it really is: this is owing to the numerous boys who accompany it, to carry the warriors' mats, mealies, gourds for holding water, and other things, and also to drive cattle for food.

The Zulus have always tried to keep on good terms with the Basutos, and their war-cry is "Silusuto," which means, "We are Basutos." They were intensely proud of having held their country against all comers, and had a saying in allusion to this, "We eat our porridge with an old spoon." Ketchwayo maintained the most rigid military discipline among his troops. I may mention the following as an example, which circumstance occurred at one of the great periodical military gatherings at Ulundi:—An Induna was making the warriors of his regiment to form line, which is often done very roughly by driving them backwards with sticks. One of the young men, the son of a chief, who had received a blow, struck the Induna in return. This did not escape the eye of the king, who, calling the man towards him, looked at him sternly, and asked him what it was that he did. He replied, "Struck the Induna,"

The Zulu War. 187

expecting to receive commendation for his boldness. The king impressively repeated the question, "What did you do?" The man returned a similar answer. The king then, with some asperity, put the same query a third time. The man now perceived that he had gone too far, and began to make excuses. Ketchwayo then remarked, glancing round at his attendants, "This man confesses that he struck an Induna, take him away,"—upon which he was immediately put to death. He would permit no disobedience of his orders, and to enforce them would resort to the most atrocious measures. On one occasion he directed a large body of young women to marry the men of one of his regiments: many of them refused, on which he despatched an Impi, or armed party, to slay them; some, having received timely warning, escaped into Natal, but large numbers were ruthlessly butchered. I have mentioned, in an early part of this work, that all the young females belonging to a man who had been "smelt out" and executed for witchcraft, became the property of the king. They were collected together in the military kraals, where they resided under the surveillance of an old woman. They were brought up with the strictest decorum in huts, quite separated from those of the men, and should it have been discovered that any intercourse had taken place between them, it would have been punished by the execution of both parties. The king selected any he might choose to be his own wives; others he sold, or compelled them to marry with his regiments. While all the Zulus greatly feared Ketchwayo, they admired and were proud of him. His voice was supreme in his councils; should all the councillors hold different opinions on a point, the king had only to give his, and every one present agreed with him, addressing him in the most flattering terms, such as lion, man-eater, father, Zulu, and so on.

There is no doubt that, for a long time previous to the outbreak of the war, the attitude of the Zulus had been extremely threatening. It was said that the young regiments were always clamouring to be allowed to "wash their spears," one of the traditional qualifications for matrimony; and to give them that opportunity they so dearly longed for, it seems that Ketchwayo requested permission from our Government to attack the Swazis, and afterwards the Boers, it is

The Zulu War.

said, but of course without effect, which caused him much annoyance. Then the old boundary dispute between the Zulus and the Boers, which we took upon ourselves by annexing the Transvaal, still rankled in the mind of every Zulu. The Sirayo affair, in which a party of armed Zulus had crossed into Natal, and carried away by force two of their refugee countrywomen, whom they afterwards slew, and the bloody raid of Umbelini across the Pongolo, showed the aggressive and truculent bearing of the Zulus towards the Government of Natal. Lastly, a Zulu Impi, composed of some 3000 men, had made a demonstration on the border: it had marched along the left bank of the Lower Tugela under the pretence of hunting, and had caused much consternation among the inhabitants of Natal, who were living near the opposite bank. It was true, as many remarked on hearing of this proceeding, that there was nothing to prevent Ketchwayo making a sudden raid across the drift, and having 30,000 men in Durban in twenty-four hours. The Zulu king evidently contemplated the possibility of a collision with the English, as he used to comfort himself with the remark " that, should they ever fight, he could do as much harm in Natal in one day as the English could do in Zululand in a year." Under such circumstances it was considered absolutely necessary to have troops stationed along the line of the frontier, and as the number of these was scarcely sufficient to guard so long a distance, a naval force was landed from H.M.S. "Active," on the 19th November, 1878, which marched to the Lower Tugela drift, where it guarded that important post until the invasion of the Zulu country by the British forces.

* * * * *

H.M.S. "Active," bearing the broad pendant of Commodore Sullivan, C.B., C.M.G., on her return from Delagoa Bay, whither she had been to communicate with the Portuguese authorities at Lorenzo Marques, anchored in the Durban roads on November 14th, 1878. The public feeling in Natal was at this time one of great insecurity. After the Zulu military demonstration which had happened some time before, an irruption into the colony was greatly dreaded, and as the number of troops for defensive purposes was certainly not superfluous, as I have said above, it was esteemed judicious to increase them as quickly as possible; and under these circumstances the commodore, not without having maturely considered the matter, and also visited the frontier, decided that a force should be landed from his flag-ship for the purpose of guarding the Lower Tugela drift and garrisoning Fort Pearson, so named after Col. Pearson of the Buffs, then just completed under the superintendence of our old comrade of the Kafir war, Lieut. Main, R.E. At noon on Tuesday, November 19th, the steamer "Forerunner" came alongside the "Active" and embarked this force; it consisted of 172 officers and men, with a Gatling and two other guns, and two rocket-tubes. The officers were Capt. H. F. Campbell in command, Lieutenants R. Craigie and W. des V. Hamilton, Surgeon W. Thompson, Lieut. T. Dowding, R.M.L.I., Sub-Lieut. C. Fraser, Mr. L. C. Coker, midshipman, Mr. J. Cotter, boatswain, and myself in medical charge. Lieut. A. B. Milne had previously landed, and was to be attached to the staff of General Lord Chelmsford as Naval Aide-de-camp. The day was bright and very hot, and those remaining on board saluted us with rounds of cheers as we steamed away, which we heartily returned, the band of the ship stationed on the poop at the same time playing several appropriate tunes. We shipped only two or three seas as we crossed the bar which separates the roadstead from the harbour of Durban, and on our arrival there we found the quay densely crowded with people, who welcomed us with vociferous cheering and waving of hats and handkerchiefs. A company of the 1st battalion, 24th regiment, had just disembarked from the "Tyne" transport, which ship had arrived in the roads during the morning, and I shook hands with my friend Lieut. Cavaye—the last time that I was ever to do so. He fell, poor fellow, shortly afterwards, fighting to the death at Isandhlwana. The commodore met us at the railway station, which was close at hand, and our messmate, the Rev. J. H. Berry, accompanied us as far as our first camping place at Smerdon's Flats, several miles from Durban, where we arrived quite safely, notwithstanding that some large stones had been placed on the rails with the object of throwing the train down a steep embankment; but they were luckily discovered by some plate-layers before the train reached the spot. The colony of Natal was suffering from a terrible drought, and all the sugar-canes in the extensive plantations through which we passed for some miles had become withered. I was told that this part of the country is exceedingly pretty during ordinary seasons, and I can easily imagine that such is the case; but as we saw it, it looked dismal in the extreme, and here and there the tall black chimney of a sugar factory only added to its dreariness. On our arrival at the Flats, where we pitched our tents for the night, we were joined by Archdeacon Lloyd of Durban, a very old resident in Natal, and who was a most genial companion. He introduced us to a small hotel in the neighbourhood, where we were furnished with a very substantial repast: during the meal he diverted us with many amusing stories of colonial life, and we were sorry when the time came for him to return to Durban.

The next morning, about six o'clock, we commenced our march, and a journey of some five miles brought us to Verulam, a small neat town, with one or two extremely good shops and numerous churches, mostly, I was informed, belonging to the Wesleyans. Immediately beyond this place we crossed the River Umhloti, where we outspanned for breakfast. The country soon became extremely pretty, green, undulating, and dotted with mimosa-trees—indeed, very much resembling the Transkei. During the afternoon we forded the Tongaati River, and encamped on the left bank, opposite a picturesquely-wooded hill, covered with trees and crowned by a ruined tower. Before turning in, we all enjoyed a bath in the clear cool stream, which was very refreshing after our hot day's journey. A thunderstorm early the next morning inaugurated a deliciously cool day; the dust was laid, and everything looked fresh and green. As we pursued our march, we found clusters of small double-white roses growing in profusion along the hedges, also brightly-tinted convolvuli, and white monopetalous flowers, with an odour like jessamine. Our next halt was near a river called the Umhlali, where there grew a number of mulberry-trees, on which our men regaled themselves. Here we were entertained by Mr. Reynolds, a large sugar-planter, who kindly invited several of us to breakfast at his charmingly situated residence. Both Mr. and Mrs. Reynolds had been to Ulundi, and had a personal interview with Ketchwayo, and they told us many stories connected with their journey. The same evening we arrived at an American mission station overlooking a broad river, the Umvoti. The missionary invited us to encamp on some of his ground, the only clear place in the neighbourhood, which was generally covered with sugar-cane.

The Zulu War.

It was raining heavily, and we stood among the long grass in our overcoats and ate our meal, which, owing to the wet, was cooked with difficulty. We crossed the river the next morning at a shallow sandy drift. A short distance beyond we met Lieut. Main, R.E., who was returning from the Lower Tugela, where he informed us he had just finished the earthwork known as Fort Pearson. Some four miles further on we passed through a small scattered place situated in a fine position on a hill, containing a few European houses, a strongly-built stone laager, to which people might fly for safety in case of necessity, and a comfortable hotel. This was Stanger, the place where the Zulu king Chaka was assassinated, and where he is buried. Beyond this the road passed through a large sugar estate, with a fine residence for the superintendent, extensive factories, and a village inhabited by the workmen, who are coolies. These natives of Hindustan are extensively employed on the sugar and other estates in Natal; they arrive in ship-loads, and are all under the surveillance of a Government inspector, who periodically visits the estates, and regular contracts are entered into between them and their employers. We next forded a river called the Nonoti, the vicinage of which is prettily wooded. We saw an alligator basking on a rock in mid-stream, which, on observing us, quietly slipped into the water. The Sinquasi was the last river we crossed. Situated some distance beyond, on a prominent hill, and environed with lofty fir-trees, was an English-looking cottage: this was known as Bleak House, and was occupied by a Mr. Charles Dickens, who was the owner of the surrounding estate.

At length, on November 24th, the Tugela, called by the Kafirs Utukela, came into view. It divides the colony of Natal from the Zulu country. It looked a very broad, turbid, winding river with a rapid current—the right, or Natal bank, covered with wood; the left, or Zulu side, being a green, open, undulating district, dotted with kraals, and entirely destitute of trees. Our road for more than a mile ran close along the river's brink, across a swampy plain covered with long grass and reeds, until we arrived opposite the drift, where there was a small hotel, kept by Mr. Smith, an old soldier of the 84th regiment. On the top of the hill immediately above us was the earthwork known as Fort Pearson, which we were to occupy; a few hundred yards to the left was a camp of a detachment of the 2nd batt., 3rd regt. ("the Buffs"), under Capt. Forster. The men turned out as we marched by, and on a soldier calling, "Three cheers for the blue-jackets," the men cheered most cordially; but their cordiality also took a more substantial shape, for they had provided two large casks of ale, which they presented to our men, and the officers had prepared quite a grand luncheon at the little hotel, to which we were invited. We pitched our camp on a grassy slope near the foot of the hill on which Fort Pearson was situated. It was evidently thought that a Zulu attack on our camp was not unlikely, and as these people usually choose the early morning for an assault, an order had been given that we were to rise regularly at 2 a.m. and get under arms, so as to be ready in case of eventualities.

On our march up I had many opportunities of hearing the opinions of the colonists as to the aspect of affairs. The vast majority appeared to be warm supporters of the policy of Sir Bartle Frere. Much as they dreaded war, they would welcome it rather than go on living in their present uncertain condition, which had existed for years, and had annually become more intolerable, until now the crisis had arrived. They considered that the most stringent terms should be imposed on Ketchwayo, which should be most implicitly fulfilled, and rather than have any "patched-up agreement," as they called it, they would prefer war. No one knew better than they did the restless condition of the young Zulu warriors, who were burning for an opportunity to blood their assegais—an appetite which must be satiated somewhere. They knew that any day the least nod from the king would slip the leash, and that forty thousand eager savages, whose pride and profession was bloodshed, would pour into Natal and butcher man, woman, and child. There was only a river to keep them slightly in check. They knew how fearfully they were outnumbered in Natal by the Kafir population, men in great part of the same race, and very frequently sympathizers with the Zulus, who, on the least success of the latter, would probably join them in the work of destruction. They were not only aware of the dissatisfaction of Ketchwayo at our holding the southern parts of the Transvaal, which he considered to be his property, but also thought how that his uncle had been autocrat of Natal, and how tempting it would be to the nephew to revive the ancient glories of his race. Besides, he had already, after a manner, commenced warfare. What else was the outrage of the sons of Sirayo ? what else that of Umbelini? what else his military demonstration on the banks of the Tugela? Sir Bartle Frere was a man equal to the occasion, and he can never attain to a higher title than that which he possesses—"The Saviour of Natal." I do not know what the ideas of the colonists were after the reverse at Isandhlwana, as I had no opportunities of judging, and it is wonderful how unstable public opinion often becomes when overshadowed by adversity; but I know that, at the period of which I am speaking, his spirited policy was the theme of general admiration along our route.

Shortly after our arrival, "the Buffs" left to join their head-quarters at "Thring's Post," a place about twenty-two miles away, and a detachment of the naval force under Lieut. Hamilton moved up and encamped in Fort Pearson, mounting our two Armstrong twelve-pounder guns so as completely to command the drift and the adjacent Zulu country, which formed part of the territory of Mr. Dunn. This drift of the Lower Tugela, some

300 yards in breadth, communicated with the most direct and main road to Ulundi, distant about 104 miles, and, when standing on Fort Pearson, it could be distinctly seen as far as a place called St. Andrew's Mission Station, some five miles off. It was this route that Mr. Shepstone and the Natal Volunteers took when they proceeded to the Amahlabatini to crown Ketchwayo. The Tugela could also be distinctly seen until it flowed into the sea a few miles below the fort, an impassable bar existing at its mouth.

During our stay at the Lower Tugela we experienced some very rainy weather, alternating with excessively hot days; on one occasion the thermometer in our tents stood at 104°, and we shifted our camp to the top of an adjacent hill, where the position was much better, the prospect finer, and where we always enjoyed a breeze. Our men soon settled down in this camp; nearly every tent had its little garden, in which radishes, mustard and cress, and other quickly-growing vegetables flourished; coops were also erected which were stocked with fowls, purchased from the neighbouring kraals; trees were cut down in the adjacent kloofs, with which sentry-boxes were built, and afterwards thatched with rushes; a shed was also put up in a similar manner, beneath a large euphorbia tree, which served as an officers' mess. The only potable water was that of the Tugela, which was very turbid.; large pits were, however, dug in the sand by the river's brink, into which the water percolated, and this was rendered additionally clear by treating it with alum, a piece of which was supplied to each tent. We formed here the acquaintance of Mr. Fynney, the Border Agent, who had a kraal near the Sinquasi River; of the Rev. Mr. Shildrick, a Church of England missionary, who had, until lately, occupied the St. Andrew's Mission Station in Zululand—things had, however, recently looked so threatening that he had received directions to leave the country; also of Dr. Jones, the district surgeon of that part of Victoria County, who resided at Stanger, which was about sixteen miles off. This latter gentleman kindly invited me to visit him, which I did, and on more than one occasion partook of the genial hospitality of Mrs. Jones and himself. Multitudes of Amatonga passed almost daily from Natal, where they had been employed as labourers, into the Zulu country on their return home; they all stopped opposite our camp, at the house of Mr. Jackson, the Tonga Agent, who registered them and examined the contents of their bundles. It was one of the stipulations between Mr. Shepstone and Ketchwayo at the coronation, that these people, who live towards Delagoa Bay, should be allowed free passage by the coast route through Zululand into Natal, and this arrangement had ever since been carried out under the supervision of Mr. John Dunn. What was the motive for this general exodus is not so easy to discover; some, perhaps, in case of war, wished to assist Ketchwayo, for their belief in his invincibility was so great that they could not imagine his being vanquished under any circumstances; others were probably uneasy as to the position of their own people, from whom, in case of war, they would have been completely cut off. We used frequently to take some very enjoyable rides about the neighbouring country, and, could the kraals have been removed, the scenery might easily have been mistaken for that of England. As a specimen of the Natal farms, I will describe one which I visited in company with my friend Dr. Jones: it was situated between our camp and

Stanger. The farmer had, some twenty-five years before, emigrated from one of our southern English counties; his farm comprised 2500 acres of capital land; he had originally obtained a free grant of 600 acres, he then got married, and his wife's dowry was 600 more, the remainder he had subsequently purchased at four shillings an acre. He lived in a house of considerable size, surrounded by several fields of arrowroot. He showed me all through his sheds and outhouses, containing machinery for crushing the tubers, and washing and drying the arrowroot starch, the whole being worked by a huge water-wheel; there was also a carpenter's and likewise a blacksmith's shop. Everything I saw had been constructed by his sons and himself, and, judging from the way in which all was finished, practice must have made them quite accomplished mechanics. The farmer likewise grew large quantities of coffee and indigo on his estate, the latter being a shrub resembling a very small laburnum; the plant, when crushed, yielding a juice which after exposure to the air, represents the indigo of commerce. He informed me that he was at that time selling his arrowroot at 40*l.* per ton, and his indigo at 8s. per pound. The labourers on his farm were all coolies from India, and there were several small houses in which they resided with their families. Near the farmhouse was a most luxuriant garden, in which everything culinary seemed to flourish. Among the fruit I particularly noticed pine-apples, paw-paws, and amatungulus. This farmer seemed to take a pride in showing us over his estate; he apologized for the absence of his ladies, who, he said, had started early that morning in a bullock-waggon for "Thring's Post," to hear the band of "the Buffs." He was evidently a man of some wealth, and had brought up his family with great respectability, and I looked on him as a fair specimen of what a poor man, who finds it difficult to live in England, and who is possessed of sobriety, perseverance, some agricultural knowledge, and who is willing to work, may become, by emigrating to a suitable colony.

It had been arranged, by means of messengers between the Natal Government and Ketchwayo, that a meeting should take place on ac ertain day at the Lower Tugela drift, between the British Commissioners and some of the Indunas representing the Zulu king and nation, when the award of the High Commissioner concerning the Transvaal boundary question, and the *ultimatum* containing the terms which the Government was resolved to enforce should be delivered verbally to the Indunas, and through them to the Zulu king. On December 9th, information was received that the chiefs had arrived at Mr. Dunn's kraal, a place about six miles off. At 8 a.m. on December 11th, our sentries on Fort Pearson reported that two or three bodies of men were advancing down the road which leads from St. Andrew's to the drift; about 10 a.m. they had arrived at the drift, and were found to be the Zulu envoys. As at this season of the year the drift is impassable, the water being deep and the current rapid, boats were sent to convey them across. There were three principal Indunas, with about fifty attendants, and all were quite unarmed. An awning had been spread under three large trees, just below Smith's Hotel, on the river's bank, and close to the drift. Beneath this the Zulus sat, in a kind of semicircle, on the ground, the Indunas being in front: these consisted of Uvumandaba, Colonel of the Umtusazwe Regiment, Umandhuli, Colonel of the Inkulutyazi Regiment, and Gebuli, a chief who had been previously employed on diplomatic missions. The first was a very fat old man, with a cruel, savage expression—on his back was a large unsightly scar, the result of a severe wound, which he was said to have received during a battle with the Boers some forty years before; the second was rather a good-looking elderly man, with a decided but not unpleasant expression; while the latter was a wiry, extremely thin little Zulu, with a remarkably keen but good-tempered cast of countenance. A table and chairs were placed for the British Commissioners, who consisted of Col. Forestier Walker, C.B., Scots Guards, and Messrs. J. Shepstone, Brownlee, and Fynn. Surrounding the whole were forty men of the Naval Brigade, without their arms, and close by were twenty-five troopers of the Stanger Mounted Rifles, under the command of Captain Addison of that corps. Several Natal chiefs were present, and were eager listeners to all which passed, as were also many of the white residents of the neighbourhood. I here, for the first time, encountered Mr. John Dunn, who had accompanied the Zulu Indunas, but in no official capacity: he is a sunburnt, good-looking man, evidently in the prime of life, and a long residence among the Zulus has in no way detracted from his gentlemanly demeanour. Mr. Fynney, the Border Agent, performed the arduous duties of interpreter, and I was told by a former resident in Zululand that he translated every expression with surprising correctness.

As a first proceeding, the award, with reference to the disputed boundary-line between Zululand and the Transvaal, was delivered, and by it the greater part of the contested territory was handed over to the Zulus. The Indunas listened with marked attention, and afterwards engaged in a long discussion; they were evidently satisfied, as they must have received back much more than they could have supposed likely; however, they did not wish that such satisfaction should be apparent, for they remarked that such a decision would "kill the heart of the king": they afterwards, however, talked with much seeming gratification to Mr. Dunn, and appeared delighted at so successful a termination of the dispute. An adjournment now took place for luncheon; a bullock was given to the Zulus, and a large quantity of sugar and water, of which they are very fond.

After about an hour had elapsed, the conference again met, and the *ultimatum* was delivered, which occupied nearly three hours. Certain points caused much consternation among the Zulu deputies, as was apparent from their faces, the expressions of which completely altered. Our demands on the Zulu king were:—

(1.) That three sons and a brother of the Induna Usirajo, or Sirayo, who, some months before, had made a raid into Natal and carried off two Zulu women, who had fled thither for protection, and whom they afterwards murdered, should be handed over to the Natal Government for trial. Similar demands had previously been made on the king, who acknowledged that such a proceeding was wrong, and sent 50*l* as compensation, which was not accepted. He was now ordered, further, to pay a fine of 500 head of cattle for the outrage and for his delay in complying with the request of our Government.

(2.) A fine of 100 head of cattle was demanded for an outrage on two British subjects at the Middle Tugela drift, about three months previously. These men were roughly seized by an armed party of Zulus,

The Zulu War.

and kept prisoners for more than two hours.

(3.) That the Swazi refugee, Umbelini, residing in the Zulu country, together with certain of his followers, to be afterwards named, should be surrendered to the Transvaal Government for trial. This man had recently made a murderous raid into that part of the disputed territory north of the Pongolo River which was claimed as British property.

(4.) That the promises made to our Government by the king and principal chiefs of the Zulu nation at the coronation, with regard to the abolition of indiscriminate bloodshed, and with reference to the institution of open trial for alleged offences, had not been carried out. These conditions were required by the British Government, in return for the support and countenance it gave to the Zulu king by sending its representative to crown him; and as the promises were openly made before the assembled Zulu people, they could not be broken without compromising the honour, dignity, and good faith of the Government. They had not been fulfilled, and the indiscriminate shedding of blood had gone on as if they had never been made. It was insisted that these promises should be rigidly carried out.

(5.) That the Zulu army should be disbanded, and should not be called out without the assent of the great council of the nation and the consent of the British Government. That the marriage laws of the country, which are part of the military system, by which men are not allowed to marry without the permission of the king, which is frequently delayed for many years, often until the men become old, should be abolished. The Zulus had no external enemies; they were surrounded on all sides by the territories of the British Government, or by those of its friends and allies; consequently their large army could only be kept up for the purpose of being used against the people of the country to which it belonged, as it constantly was, or else against the peaceful British possessions around, and it was impossible for any people to feel secure when they were constantly menaced by, and in danger of aggression from, the Zulu army.

(6.) That a British Resident should be appointed, who should live in the Zulu country, or on its immediate border, who was to be a medium for all communications

The Zulu War.

between the two Governments, and who would see that all these enactments were properly carried out.

(7.) Panda had allowed several missionaries to settle in Zululand, but Ketchwayo had killed some of the natives living at the mission stations, and had so terrified the remainder that the missionaries had been obliged to withdraw. It was now required that the missionaries should be allowed to return, and that, if a Zulu wished to listen to them, he should be permitted to do so.

Ketchwayo, it is well known, always had an antipathy to missionaries, and one of his favourite sayings in connexion with them was, that "a Christian Zulu is a spoiled Zulu."

The cattle fines were to be paid within twenty days, and the word of the king as to his acquiescence in the imposed terms was to be given within thirty days.

The delivery of the *ultimatum* having been concluded, the Zulu deputies, whose countenances had become somewhat rueful, had a short and evidently very earnest consultation together. They then said that they had a message from the king, which was, that "he had faithfully carried out all his coronation engagements;" they also said that the stipulations of Somtsen at the coronation had been carried out, and I saw them produce a piece of paper on which I understood that the articles of that agreement were written. They stated that the Zulu people had declared on that occasion, with regard to the stopping of bloodshed, that they would kill (1) any one having intercourse with the king's women; (2) any one who stole the royal cattle; (3) any man or woman who committed adultery. (4) With regard to the stipulation that any persons accused of witchcraft should be given a further trial, but that if they continued in their evil courses they should be put to death, the deputies remarked that they could not help killing people for witchcraft, but that they were always given three chances: the accused was first sent to a kraal in another part of the country; if again accused, he was moved a second and a third time; and if, after that, he still persisted, the Induna Gebuli asked, in a desponding tone, "What else are we to do?" They added also that, as the English kept up an army in Natal, they could not see why they should not be permitted to do so in the Zulu country. Two copies of the *ultimatum* were handed over to them for delivery to the king—the one written in English, the other in Zulu. They then requested that some British representative should accompany them to communicate such very serious demands to the king. During the conference, one or two of the Zulus moved their seats and created some little confusion. Mr. Shepstone, however, severely censured them for the interruption, and impressed on the Zulus generally the gravity of the situation. The bearing of the Zulu Indunas was on the whole dignified, collected, and courteous, without the least exhibition of temper or bravado. During the conference, Mr. Lloyd, a photographer from Durban, photographed the scene. Uvumundaba, casually looking up, observed the camera directed at him. He seemed very disconcerted, and muttered something to Umandhuli, who was sitting next him: he likewise appeared much disturbed, which Mr. Shepstone observing, immediately explained the innocent nature of the operation. When the interview was over, several people present, who could speak Kafir, talked with the Indunas: they appeared very agreeable in conversation, and even polished in manner, with the exception of Uvumundaba, who was either of a morose, retiring disposition, or his discomposure was too great to permit of his talking. Shortly after 5 p.m. they were conveyed to the Zulu side of the river in boats. Many were the opinions expressed by the colonists as to the effect of this *ultimatum* on Ketchwayo: most people seemed to think that he would pay the cattle, and then, after a great deal of haggling, would accede to all the terms; but one or two old residents among the Zulus, who knew Ketchwayo personally, gave it as their opinion that "he would not listen to any of the demands for a moment."

For some time afterwards our men were actively employed, under the direction of Lieut. Main, R.E., in putting together the pont or floating bridge for transporting troops across the Tugela, the materials for which had been sent from Durban. On Christmas Day all the tents in the Naval Brigade camp were decorated with evergreens, and the men had a plentiful supply of plum-pudding, which had been kindly sent them by Mr Jameson, a merchant of Durban. In the afternoon several of the officers went to a buck hunt, and in the evening we all dined together in a marquee, the Rev. J. H. Berry, our chaplain, having come from Durban to spend a few days with us. Sub-Lieut. J. Heugh, of the "Active," was also present, having come to join the Naval Brigade. The next day our athletic sports were held, the prizes having been raised by subscription. A few days afterwards Commodore Sullivan arrived, as did also General Lord Chelmsford, accompanied by Lieut. Milne, Naval A.D.C. They held a minute inspection of the Naval Brigade, and delivered some eulogistic speeches; they likewise directed some important additions to be made to the defences of Fort Pearson. When the commodore left, all the officers went to Smith's hotel to wish him good-bye: we gave him three ringing cheers as he drove away, and we were all very sorry to lose him. On the last day of the year 1878, the time allowed to the Zulu king for the payment of the cattle having expired, Mr. John Dunn's people, with all their cattle and movable property, began to evacuate their territory and to cross the Tugela into Natal. He had been requested by Ketchwayo to remain quietly in his own district, as he would soon settle the English, or, to render his expression literally, "would cut us up like little bits of meat": but Mr. Dunn had held a personal interview with the General during his visit to the Lower Tugela, and had ascertained that, were he to remain in the Zulu country, no guarantee could be given that he would not be molested when our troops should cross the river. Some Zulu chiefs had also come to see the General, one of whom begged most piteously that more time should be allowed to settle affairs, and asked, "Can nothing be done to stay proceedings?" But the General at once saw through his motives, and answered decisively that "in a couple of months or so their mealies would be ripe, and then they would be secure with regard to food, and did they think him such a fool as to permit them to do this?" This speech acted like an electric shock; they saw that the game was up, and departed without another word. A report came on New Year's Eve that a Zulu Impi of ten or twelve thousand men had arrived some ten miles off, and it was believed that their orders were to attack our camp. This was rather serious news, as we had only 160 men in all; however, we had a fine position within Fort Pearson to retreat to in case of a reverse. Communication was at once cut off at the drift, extra sentries posted at the fort, round the camp, and along the river, with orders to fire on the occurrence of the least suspicious movement, and we all slept in our clothes, with our arms ready; but no alarm occurred.

On New Year's Day, 1879, the telegraph between Maritzburg and Fort Pearson was completed, under the superintendence of Mr. Sievwright, director of telegraphs; the Kafir labourers, who had been employed at the work, giving three cheers, like Englishmen, as the last wire was connected. The exodus of Mr. Dunn's people went on daily: on one day 2500 cattle and about 1000 people crossed the Tugela. It was very interesting to watch them congregating on the green slopes opposite, preparatory to being conveyed across in boats. The cattle all swam the river, the drivers swimming with them. Two of these men were drowned, but their people did not seem to think much of it. One of the bodies was washed up on the bank, but it was thrown again into the river, and the current probably conveyed it quickly to the alligators. Dunn's Zulus, as they crossed, all bivouacked just above the drift: they divided themselves into small bodies, each one surrounding itself with a ring fence, formed of the branches of trees, to protect them from the wind: in the centre of each enclosure was a large fire, around which the Zulus sat, and looked very happy. Each man, as he arrived on the Natal side of the river, delivered his fire-arms to Mr. Fynney and his police. When every one had crossed, all the people started for the country near Mr. Fynney's kraal, where they were to be located. The procession reminded me strongly of the Biblical pictures of Abraham and the old patriarchs: there was Mr. Dunn, with his wives and concubines, his wild-looking men, armed with spears, driving forwards the flocks and herds—his women and children, many hundreds in number, carrying their mats and cooking utensils on their heads, and the mothers with their little ones at their backs—a pastoral people migrating from one district to another.

The 2nd regiment of the Natal Native Contingent, consisting of two battalions, each 1100 strong, under the command of Major Graves, of "the Buffs," assembled within a few miles of us, close to the Nonoti River, where they underwent daily drill; and the Natal Native Pioneers, a small corps of Kafir Sappers, and

The Zulu War.

an extremely fine body of men, 100 strong, dressed in the Royal Engineer uniform, and commanded by Capt. Beddoes, encamped close to us.

On January 4th our men successfully launched the pont, and, under the direction of the officers of the Naval Brigade, a steel hawser was subsequently stretched across the river and made fast to either bank. The pont was fastened to this by means of sliding ropes, technically known as "lizards," the motive power on each side being, at first, companies of the Native Contingent, afterwards spans of oxen. This pont could convey from 80 to 100 men at each trip, or a heavily-laden waggon with a span of oxen. It was worked by a party of our sailors and marines, under the orders of Mr. Cotter, boatswain; and the care and celerity with which he afterwards conducted the transit of the invading force was the subject of general commendation.

I went down to the river to witness the launch, and met Mr. Dunn, who told me that he had frightened the Zulus by saying that the ships-of-war would probably land large forces on their coast; that now the Zulus, who were his neighbours, saw that he had left his district, they were all "treking" northwards; and that he did not think that there would be much fighting, as there was a strong peace party in the country. He also said that Ketchwayo would not be able to bring more than 30,000 fighting men into the field, about a third of whom possessed fire-arms, "the musket barrels being mostly gas-pipes," to quote his words. Shortly after the pont was afloat, a party being at work on board, Lieut. Craigie and D. Martin, A.B., were accidentally precipitated into the water. The latter was drowned, his body being carried away by the rapid current. Two blue-jackets gallantly jumped in to save him, regardless of the alligators, both of whom were afterwards awarded the Royal Humane Society's medal. Lieut. Craigie, having been carried beneath the pont, had a very narrow escape. On January 4th the 2nd battalion of "the Buffs," about 800 strong, under Lieut.-Col. Parnell, came and encamped near us; and, on the 6th, a company of forty blue-jackets from H.M.S. "Tenedos" arrived, under Lieut. Kingscote, with Staff-Surgeon Longfield in medical charge. They took up their quarters in Fort Pearson, the men of the "Active" being withdrawn, as, after their former experience in Kafir warfare, they were considered to be particularly adapted for forming a part of the column which was shortly to invade the Zulu country under Col. Pearson. It was decided that this force should cross the Tugela on the 10th and following days, the 10th being the day on which the time allowed to Ketchwayo to comply with the terms of the *ultimatum* would expire, and that then it should push on as rapidly as possible and seize and fortify Ekowe, a Norwegian mission station thirty-seven miles distant, so that stores might be collected there, and that it might serve as a base for further operations. For some three or four days previous to the passage of the river, numerous Zulus had been seen roaming about the country opposite, for the purpose of plundering John Dunn's abandoned kraals. On one occasion a shell was fired at them from our 12-pounder Armstrong: it burst above a large group of Zulus, and soon caused them to disappear over a ridge.

By the 15th all the troops had crossed, including the Natal native regiment—and very well it looked, each man wearing a blue blanket with a scarlet fillet round the head; only twenty men in every hundred, however, were provided with fire-arms. A large camp was formed on the left bank of the Tugela.

Crowds of the colonists flocked to the right bank to witness the crossing, taking possession of every point from which a view could be obtained; the scene having much the appearance of a gigantic picnic. During the time we remained in this camp, Capt. Barrow, 19th Hussars, who commanded the mounted infantry and the Natal Volunteer Horse, made two cavalry reconnaissances—on one occasion penetrating some ten miles into the country. He observed about a dozen Zulus on a hill, and was on them so quickly that the men threw away their guns and assegais, so as to run the faster: he, however, took five prisoners, one of whom, on being captured, observed, "It is very fine, a hundred or two of you assailing half a dozen men; only wait till you get further on, then you'll find something for you." About 50 Zulu men, women, and children, bringing 40 assegais and 1 gun, came in and surrendered: among them was a witch doctor, a man of a most repulsive aspect.

The majority of the European troops in camp was employed in throwing up a large rectangular earthwork: they certainly toiled

The Zulu War. 223

very hard in the burning sun, so as to complete it with all despatch. After the column had marched, it was occupied in part by the naval contingent of H.M.S. "Tenedos," who added some improvements, and named it Fort Tenedos, after their ship.

At 6 a.m. on January 18th, the march into Zululand was commenced, the column consisting of two parts, the advanced division comprising the following numbers:—

Naval Brigade, H.M.S. "Active," Capt. H. F. Campbell, R.N.	172
2nd Battalion, "the Buffs". Lieut.-Col. Parnell.	783
Royal Engineers Capt. Wynne, R.E.	104
Royal Artillery Lieut. Lloyd, R.A.	30
Cavalry Capt. Barrow, 19th Hussars.	190
Various departments	12
1st Batt., 2nd Natal Native Regt. Major Graves.	1100
	2391

The Naval Brigade was provided with two 7-pounder guns, one Gatling gun, and two rocket-tubes; the Royal Artillery had likewise two 7-pounder guns.

The strength of the second, or rear division,

which followed a short distance behind the first, was :—

>99th Regiment 580
>   Lieut.-Col. Welman.
>Cavalry 184
>   Capt. Addison, Natal Horse.
>Natal Native Pioneers 102
>   Capt. Beddoes.
>2nd Batt., 2nd Natal Native Regt. 1140
>   Commandant Nettleton.
>
>   ———
>   2006

The entire strength of the column was therefore 2055 white troops and 2342 natives, forming a total of 4397. This column was under the command of Col. Pearson, formerly of "the Buffs." Col. Walker, C.B., Scots' Guards, was Staff-officer, and Capt. McGregor, 29th regiment, Quartermaster-General. The medical officers included Surgeon-Major Fitzmaurice, A.M.D., Surgeon Thompson, R.N., Civil Surgeons Mansell and Giles, and myself. The commissariat was in charge of Commissary Heygate, while the Rev. Mr. Robertson, the well-known Zulu missionary, was attached to the column as chaplain and political agent. The cavalry was composed in part of the different troops of the Natal Volunteer Horse, and in part of

The Zulu War.

mounted infantry. Above 100 waggons accompanied the column.

We outspanned for breakfast at St. Andrew's about 9 a.m., in a drizzling rain, and afterwards passed through a perfectly open country without seeing a single Zulu, and crossed a small river known as the Inyoni, above which we encamped for the night among some very high, wet grass.

The next day was bright and clear, and I looked down on what appeared like a vast green park, gently undulating, thickly studded with mimosas, a flashing stream winding across it, with the distant glittering sea on the one hand, and a lovely blue headland on the other, some twenty miles off, and towering above the Tugela. One could scarcely realize that this was the scene of that savage and bloody combat between the Zulu factions in 1856. Our progress to-day was very slow, owing to the great length of the column, and the heavy, slippery condition of the road, several halts having to be made to permit the second half of the force to come up. We crossed the Umsundusi River at 4 p.m., and encamped a short distance beyond; part of the column had, however, to bivouac on the other side. During the night, some men of our native regiment, having observed some Zulus about a kraal on a neighbouring hill, rushed up and set it on fire; and as the cause of this conflagration was not known in the camp, the Naval Brigade was under arms half the night. I walked through the camp of the native regiment, which consisted of several parallel rows of branches fixed firmly in the ground, so as to form a series of green walls to keep off the wind: against these their arms were placed, and between them were lines of fires, where they roasted their meat and mealies. The native soldiers must have been up very early, as shortly after sunrise they were to be seen coming towards the camp from all quarters, laden with green mealies, fowls, and pumpkins, which they had "looted," their faces beaming with satisfaction. My horse had been ailing since we left the Tugela, and I asked Mr. Robertson, who has had great experience in such matters in this country, to examine him. He said that he had an inflammatory affection of the mouth, called "Lampers." He then freely incised the part with a penknife and rubbed in salt, kindly lending me one of his animals until mine recovered, which he did after this treatment in a few days.

The Zulu War.

Our next advance was through a district where large numbers of pumpkins grew, many of which our men placed on the waggons. We crossed the Amatakulu River, and passed for a considerable distance through very dense bush: it was thought that a Zulu army might be awaiting us here, and it was consequently searched by several companies of troops before the waggons crossed the drift. This drift had been examined the day before by the Royal Engineers, who had advanced so far accompanied by an adequate force, and stakes had been driven into the bed of the river, so as to mark the line at which the waggons were to cross. The Royal Engineers and Natal Native Pioneers, after the cavalry had gone ahead, marched well in advance of the column, so as to mend the road, cut down trees, and remove any object likely to cause delay. We outspanned at some distance beyond the Amatakulu, while a force, consisting in part of the Naval Brigade, made a detour of some three miles to attack the district military kraal of 'Mkinkinlhovu, better known now as Ginginlhovo: it was found deserted, and was set on fire. In one kraal a very old woman was found. On being questioned, she stated that everybody had left the neighbourhood, and there were no troops anywhere. Our experiences in the Kafir war led us to doubt this statement. She was taken charge of by Mr. Robertson, who placed her in his waggon.

The morning of the next day, January 22nd, was lovely. We started from our camping ground at 5 a.m., passing through a low-lying, rather swampy country, covered with mealies. There was a prominent hill a few miles in advance, on the summit of which were seen some half-dozen Zulus: our cavalry was well in front, and it was hoped that they might be captured. About 8 a.m., having crossed the Inyezane River, we had come to the foot of the hill which formed the commencement of the mountainous country in which Ekowe is situated. Here the road took a somewhat semicircular sweep up a hill, and this was commanded on either side by one of much greater height, the bases of which were covered with thin bush. Here we were about to outspan; the cavalry had already unsaddled, and part of the Natal native regiment had passed some distance up the road. I had ridden part of the way up the hill, engaged in conversation with Capt. McGregor, when we suddenly heard heavy firing a short distance above us. This was from our advanced cavalry and the Natal native regiment, and we immediately perceived that we were partly surrounded by a large force of Zulus. As we were conspicuous objects, from being on horseback, we were evidently specially aimed at, bullets whistling by us as we thought in very close proximity. I looked round and saw the Zulus on our right, running like deer, in a long semicircle: this was the right horn of their army, trying to surround the first part of our column and cut the line of the waggons. Col. Pearson and his staff now posted themselves on a knoll, a little to the right of the road, and with them was part of the Naval Brigade, with the rocket-tubes, two companies of "the Buffs," and the artillery, with two 7-pounder guns; and these commenced the action with the chest or main body of the army, the fire soon becoming extremely hot. "The Buffs" were extended in skirmishing order to defend the front, and the Naval Brigade, after doing great execution from its position in advance, was ordered to move up the road—a work of much difficulty, as a heavy fire was poured into it from three sides by the Zulus on the heights above, wounding four of the blue-jackets. There was a kraal towards the top of the hill, on the left of the road, which was stubbornly held by a strong body of the enemy, forming the left horn of the Zulu army; but the rocket party of the Naval Brigade, under Mr. Cotter, boatswain, having sent a rocket right through one of the huts, set the kraal on fire. The Natal native regiment then advanced and drove out the Zulus, taking possession of the kraal. The Naval Brigade continued to advance with great intrepidity, but their fire seemed to have no effect in dislodging the Zulus from the ridges in front. It was then determined to make a charge up the hill and along the ridges. At this time the blue-jackets were reinforced by a company of "the Buffs," under Lieut.-Col. Parnell, whose horse was immediately shot under him. Capt. Campbell, commanding the Naval Brigade, behaved with much gallantry : he called to the men to follow him and close with the enemy, and then, accompanied by Capt. Hart, staff-officer of the Natal native regiment, an officer of unflinching courage, galloped towards the Zulu position. The A company of the Naval Brigade, under Lieut. Hamilton, followed as quickly as possible, and the B company, under

Sub-Lieut. Fraser, was not far behind. The Zulus seemed bewildered by this determined advance; they wavered and then bolted to a man, while the blue-jackets rapidly advanced and occupied the heights—the first man in the enemy's position being an ordinary seaman called Harding. This was the crowning act of the engagement, inasmuch as it drove back the chest, or main body, of the Zulu army. The Gatling gun, under Mr. Coker, midshipman, was brought to the front about this time; but as this weapon, together with the Marines under Lieut. Dowding, was in rear of the waggons, it was some time before they could get into action. The right horn of the Zulu army was met by a company of "the Buffs," and by the Royal Engineers under Capt. Wynne, who first checked its advance, and then slowly but determinedly drove it back, following it in skirmishing order through the bush for a long distance. One of the rocket-tubes of the Naval Brigade, and the guns of the Royal Artillery posted on the knoll, played on part of the chest of the Zulu army, and on the right horn, some of the shells bursting with great accuracy. The Zulus at length began to give way generally, and after the fight had lasted for nearly three hours, they retired over the hills in comparatively good order. The hospital ambulance was placed a little to the left of the road, and, as must always be the case when attacked by an army in the Zulu formation, was in the centre of the fire; luckily the enemy, as a rule, fired high, and although the vehicle was repeatedly hit, no one was injured. Civil Surgeon Mansell, and latterly Surgeon Thompson, R.N., were most assiduous in attending to the wounded, which, although generally thought lightly of, is practically no light matter, when it is considered that in the heat of action, whilst all around are filled with excitement, a man has to be cool, to remember his anatomy, and to do his duty with a steady hand and a clear head. The casualties among the white troops in this action were 2 officers, 4 non-commissioned officers, and 3 men killed, and 15 wounded, 7 of the latter belonging to the Naval Brigade.

The Zulu position was a very strong one, chosen with great judgment, and it completely commanded the road for a considerable distance. Their army was lying in ambush, and as it was evident that we should either come to a halt or ascend the hill very slowly, their intention was suddenly to surprise us, had they not been prematurely discovered by the Natal Native Contingent. The Zulus lost above 300 killed in this action, which is known as the Battle of Inyezane. They were commanded by the Induna Godidi, and their strength, as we ascertained from a prisoner we took, was about 5000 men, although from other sources we heard that it was about 8000. The prisoner stated that the army was composed as follows:—

Umdhluefu regiment . . . . . . 1000 in number.
Umxapu ,, (*i. e.* " the Sprinklers ") 2000 ,,
'Ngulubi ,, (*i. e.* " the Pigs.") 500 ,,
District military kraals:
  Ginginlhovo ⎫
  Isigwaka   ⎪
  Umangwe   ⎬ about . . . . 1500 ,,
  Umkandhlu   ⎭

Total, 5000

On our side about 600 white troops and the greater part of the 1st battalion of the Natal native regiment were engaged. The bodies of one of the officers and one of the non-commissioned officers killed were covered with assegai wounds. A large grave was dug under some trees to the left of the road, in which the bodies of our slain were placed, the funeral service being read over them by Mr. Robertson. Capt. Gelston, of "the Buffs," after our arrival at Ekowe, made a wooden cross, on which he carved an inscription, and it was placed over this grave by the first convoy which left for the Lower Tugela. Immediately that the battle was over, and the wounded had been placed in appropriate vehicles, the column continued its march, in order that the enemy should not suppose that we had received a check. The solitary prisoner we took had been wounded in the leg. Our Natal Kafirs clamoured to be allowed to put him to death, according to their custom, but this was, of course, not permitted. He informed us that they had received positive orders from Ketchwayo, who knew the locality well, to attack us in this place, which, besides affording them a splendid position, was a spot where they had been victorious on a former occasion—a matter to which they attach great importance. He was asked why he fought against us when the Zulu people well knew that our quarrel was not with them, but with their ruler. He answered somewhat nobly, as I thought, "And what would you think of a people which would desert their king?" His wounds were attended to, and he was taken on under a guard: he belonged to the Tulwana regiment. On the top of the hill we passed the corpses of several Zulus, some of which were terribly burned, probably by the Naval Brigade rockets. We procceded for some four miles along a difficult country, thick bush existing on either side of the road, which was very hilly; and now that we had been attacked by a Zulu army, we burned all the kraals on our route, an act which we had sedulously avoided before, to show that our quarrel was with the king only, the military kraal of Ginginlhovo being royal property. We finally bivouacked on a lofty position, above a stream of excellent water.

About noon of the next day we arrived at Ekowe, the road taking a very circuitous route of some six miles, part of which passed through the Hintza forest. Could we have gone in a direct line, the distance would probably not have been more than half. We saw the place above us for a long time before we reached it, and on our arrival found that the Zulus had not molested it in any way; everything appeared to be intact; indeed, as I afterwards ascertained, a neighbouring chief had directed one of his men to take care of it. This was the station of the Rev. Mr. Oftebro, a Norwegian missionary. It consisted of a neat brick-built church, with a vestry attached, and having a small tower, the whole roofed with corrugated iron; a long building, containing several rooms, one of which had been used as a school; and a third building, with a verandah, which was Mrs. Oftebro's private residence: both the latter were covered with a neat reed thatch. In front of the residence was a magnificent garden, through which ran a fine avenue of orange trees, leading down to a stream of the clearest running water, which had its source in a spring about 200 yards distant. Situated about 300 yards off, on the south and east, were two small cottages. This mission station, properly called Etshowye, although generally marked on the charts as Ekowe, was situated on an extensive plateau nearly 2000 feet above the sea level, and was commanded on every side except the south-west by low hills, distant only from three to four hundred yards. Some 1700 yards to the south was a high, rocky ridge, which we afterwards named Observatory Hill, because from it could be obtained an extensive view of the whole coast country, from the lagoon at the mouth of the Umslatoosi to far beyond the Tugela, which river, as the crow flies, was about twenty-nine miles distant. The entire district was covered with grass, and contained several springs; indeed, this undulating plateau of Ekowe appeared to be the watershed of numerous streams, besides the Umlalazi River, which could be traced below, meandering for some sixteen or eighteen miles through long, woody ravines, until it reached the sea. The hills around Ekowe were destitute of trees, which, however, grew in profusion along many of the valleys. This mission station must have been a pleasant abode when occupied and under cultivation. At the time of our arrival, however, it was covered with long rank grass and overgrown vegetation, which afforded shelter to numerous snakes, especially to puff adders, which were so very common that they were occasionally killed either within or close to one's tent of a morning. Around the church was a small grave-yard, containing only two or three graves, in one of which, marked by a large granite cross, were interred the remains of Mrs. Robertson, the late wife of our chaplain, who had been accidentally killed near Ekowe some years previously.

Shortly after our arrival a Zulu came in with a flag of truce and surrendered himself. The tents of the various corps were pitched around this mission station, and in front of each camp a shelter trench was dug in case of attack. The next day the officers of the Royal Engineers were busily occupied in tracing out the lines for the earthworks which were to enclose the church, school, and mission house. During the night a mad Zulu, whom Mr. Robertson had met in the day, and had allowed to go, returned to the camp, and was fired on by a sentry: the "alert" was immediately sounded, and everybody stood to his arms.

On the 25th a large number of empty waggons left for the Lower Tugela, with an escort of several companies of "the Buffs," and of the 99th regiment, under Major Coates, to bring up fresh supplies, which it would be necessary to store in large quantities at Ekowe before a further advance could be made. The earthworks were commenced; the men, although baking in the sun, worked most energetically.

26th.—Two native runners arrived from the Tugela with a despatch, stating that Col. Durnford had been killed, and his column of natives cut to pieces. A report arrived at the same time from Lieut. Kingscote, R.N., commanding at Fort Tenedos, that an attack had been made by the Zulus on that position on the night of the 25th; heavy firing was kept up from the fort, but that no dead or wounded Zulus could be discovered in the morning, as the enemy had probably dragged them away. The 28th of January was an eventful day at Ekowe. The night before, the camp had just settled down to sleep, when two rifle-shots were heard near, and some of the Natal native outposts reported that the Zulu army was assembling on the surrounding hills. The "alert" was sounded, and, after being under arms for about an hour, the alarm was found to be false. About 10 a.m. a runner arrived bearing a despatch from Lord Chelmsford to Col. Pearson, which said—"You may expect the whole Zulu army upon you; consider all former orders cancelled, and take the best steps you can for the safety of your column. If you are not in a position to remain at Ekowe, retire at once and hold the line of the Tugela." It was also stated that the General's column had been defeated by the Zulus, that he had fallen back across the Tugela, and Col. Wood on Utrecht, and that ours was the only column in the Zulu country. It was decided that we should fall back at once on the Tugela, taking only rations and ammunition for three days, and that the tents and waggons should be burned. Shortly afterwards, however, these orders were rescinded, principally owing to the fact that Lieut.-Col. Eley, of the 99th, was ascertained to be only a few miles distant with the first of the convoys bringing provisions; so that it was now decided to proceed with the fortifications as rapidly as possible, and hold the fort as long as the provisions could be made to last. It now became important that no more men should be kept at Ekowe than were absolutely necessary for maintaining the position. Consequently, the Natal native regiment, the Natal Volunteer Horse, and the mounted infantry, were sent back to the Lower Tugela, being ordered to make a forced march; they left early the same afternoon, Lieut. Courtenay, 20th Hussars, kindly taking charge of our hastily-written letters. The men set to work with alacrity to complete the earthworks; all our baggage, boxes of biscuit, bags of mealies, tents, tent-bags filled with earth, and even articles of clothing, rolled up, were placed together to form temporary defences. The church and vestry were loop-holed, and all the outlying tents removed to within the enclosure. The four 7-pounder guns, two of which belonged to the Naval Brigade, the Gatling, and rocket-tubes were placed in position. The church tower, from which a very extensive general view could be obtained, was used as a "look-out," and one of our signalmen, with his telescope, was stationed therein. I placed all the sick and wounded on stretchers inside the church, which I fitted up as a hospital, having had several holes cut near the ground to increase the ventilation. Everything available which could possibly be made to hold water was filled, in case the Zulus should contaminate the spring, or temporarily cut us off from it; and, during the whole time that we held the position, barrels were always kept filled, in view of a similar emergency. The convoy arrived about 7 p.m., although seven waggons filled with commissariat stores had to be abandoned on the road. We were now reinforced by three companies of the 99th regiment.

30th.—The men were still toiling hard at the earthworks, and we were now so efficiently entrenched that many were heard to express a wish that the Zulus would "come on." 650 trek oxen, which Col. Pearson decided to send back to the Lower Tugela, so as to economize the pasturage as much as possible, left this morning. They were all captured by the Zulus after they had proceeded a few miles, the drivers escaping with difficulty. These men ascertained that the Zulus had plundered the waggons which had been abandoned, and then tried to burn them, the stores they contained having been strewed all over the place. Some runners were sent to the Tugela, but they likewise returned, saying that they could not get beyond the Inyezane, as the Zulus "were like the grass."

Feb. 2nd.—Bodies of the enemy had been seen at some distance for the last two or three days. On one occasion they sat along the ridge of the Observatory Hill, watching the fort; but they were dislodged by some shell, admirably directed by Lieut. Lloyd, R.A. The rapid ringing of the church bell, swung on a wooden frame in the middle of the fort, was the alarm signal; and this bell generally roused up every one once or twice every night. A messenger arrived from the

The Zulu War.

Lower Tugela, after running great risks: he brought the mournful particulars of the disaster at Isandhlwana, which took place on the same day as our engagement at Inyezane. Nearly all our old friends of the Kafir war, belonging to the 1st battalion of the 24th, had been killed. There were many cloudy brows in the fort to-day, and many were the vows of vengeance on the Zulus should they pay us a visit. During several succeeding days a runner occasionally arrived, and others were despatched to the Lower Tugela, some of whom probably lost their lives. Large numbers of Zulus, carrying white shields, were seen going in the direction of the Inyezane.

The garrison of Ekowe was composed of the following troops:—Naval Brigade, H.M.S. "Active," under Capt. Campbell; 2nd company of Royal Engineers, Capt. Wynne; a few Royal Artillery, Lieut. Lloyd; six companies of "the Buffs," Lieut.-Col. Parnell; and three companies of the 99th, Lieut.-Col. Welman; forming a total of 1397 Europeans. There were, besides, the Natal Native Pioneers, under Capt. Beddoes, and numerous native drivers, forming a grand total of 1858. Col. Pearson was in command; Col. Walker, C.B., Scots' Guards, staff-officer; Capt. McGregor, 29th regiment, Quartermaster-general; the transport was under Capt. Pelly Clarke, 103rd Fusiliers, and Lieut. Thirkill, 88th regiment; Rev. Mr. Robertson was the Church of England, and Rev. Mr. Welsh, the Roman Catholic, chaplain; the commissariat was under Commissary Heygate, and the medical department under myself.

11*th*.—Runners arrived from the General, saying that it was impossible that he could advance again for a considerable time, and directing Col. Pearson to return to the Lower Tugela with what was styled the "surplus" garrison. It was proposed that the Naval Brigade, with one gun, the Royal Engineers, the three companies of the 99th, and the Natal Pioneers, should return by a night march across country, under the guidance of one of Mr. Robertson's men; but this proposition was never carried out. The Zulus soon became very annoying, firing on our cattle-drivers, and on the videttes when they were posted of a morning; these latter consisting of a few Natal volunteers who had been left behind, and infantry mounted on the officers' horses. Their posts were a few hundred yards distant from the fort, the most advanced being the one on the Observatory Hill, and from these posts they periodically patrolled the ridges, and watched the entire neighbourhood; they were, of course, withdrawn as it began to get dark. These were under the command of Lieut. Rowden, of the 99th.

24th.—The fort may now be said to have been in a complete state of defence; a ditch, seven feet deep by ten feet wide, entirely surrounded it, besides a broad earthwork, several feet in height. Although, up to the day that the fort was evacuated, improvements were constantly going on, caponniéres were built, the ditches planted with sharp stakes, draw-bridges made, strong traverses formed with sods, and wire entanglements laid down outside the fort. Rows of waggons were arranged a short distance inside the earthworks, underneath which the men lived, the wind and rain being kept out by tarpaulins; the waggons themselves were piled with bags of earth and other things, to act as traverses. The timber in the near kloofs was all felled and the ground cleared, the two cottages outside the fort demolished, and everything swept away which would afford the least cover to the enemy; the distances of all the neighbouring ridges were measured and staked, so as to insure accuracy of fire. All the cooking was carried on outside the fort, and the horses, with the exception of those belonging to the staff, were stabled in one of the ditches. The oxen were at first kept at night within a laager of waggons in a small ravine, well under the fire of the fort—latterly large numbers of them were nocturnally driven into one of the ditches: by day they were sent out to graze, two or three companies of troops being placed beyond them as a guard. The pasturage near the fort was very soon consumed, and the cattle had sometimes to be driven out for a considerable distance, becoming every week perceptibly leaner. Strong parties of troops occasionally made short excursions, burnt the neighbouring kraals, and collected mealies and pumpkins. Distant Zulus would sometimes shout to our natives on these occasions, "If you come and eat our pumpkins, we'll come into Ekowe and drink your coffee;" and they would also call to our cattle-drivers, who were looking after our oxen, "Mind and take care of our king's cattle, we're soon coming for them," or "We're coming on at you the day after to-morrow." The Kafirs regard the new moons as auspicious occasions, and when these occurred we confidently expected an attack.

Towards the end of February a great deal of sickness began to be present in the fort, principally remittent fever and dysentery, which was not to be wondered at when we consider the circumstances which obtained there. The soil at Ekowe was of an unhealthy nature, and the spot never would have been selected as a site for a permanent camp by any one versed in sanitary science, but it was imperative that this consideration should yield to military necessity. The upper portion, about two feet thick, consisted of black mould, formed by the consecutive decay of many generations of grasses, and large quantities of other vegetable matter; beneath this was a stratum of sand, some four inches in thickness, also containing organic matter; and then came several feet of soft clay, in which water could easily be obtained by digging. The extensive ditch by which the fort was surrounded did a great deal towards draining it, and, moreover, the ground had a gentle slope towards the eastward; but a soil consisting almost entirely of vegetable matter placed over a watery subsoil in so hot a climate could not be healthy. The wet season was also at its height, and the ground became saturated every few days, and then a burning sun would cause a copious exhalation. The men lived and slept beneath the shelters formed of the waggon tarpaulins, which consisted of oiled canvas, and these, besides being water-proof, were also air-proof. The result was that the malarious emanations from the ground could not escape, and these becoming mingled with the exhalations from the bodies of men, so closely packed together, produced a poisonous atmosphere, which they sometimes inhaled for days together. Other causes of sickness were, the very heavy work which was required of the men under a broiling sun, when on a reduced scale of diet; the alternations of heat and cold, the thermometer standing one day at 97°, and the next at 67°, with fogs and rain; and, lastly, exposure—men at their posts frequently lying in the mud the greater part of the night, with the rain pouring on them, and without any protection beyond their overcoats. The cases of purely typhoid fever at Ekowe were undoubtedly caused by some soldiers belonging to a working party having foolishly filled their water-bottles at a small stream which flowed directly from the cemetery, and which also drained the ground that was set aside for the burial of the dead bullocks. The supply of medicines allowed to the column was soon expended, and had I not requisitioned the boxes of horse medicine, which contained a few very useful drugs, and utilized the bark of the water-boom tree which grew near, and which I found to contain powerfully astringent qualities, the mortality would have been much greater. A shed was erected on the top of a neighbouring hill, and to this the sick were removed every morning, and allowed to remain till towards evening, so that the fresh air might constantly blow over them; and this I am convinced saved many lives, and it moreover permitted the church to be completely cleansed and ventilated daily. An efficient guard always surrounded it. There were twenty-eight deaths during our detention at Ekowe, twenty-five of them being from disease. Visiting the hospital was often most painful; all the occupants were dangerously ill, and their moans were heartrending. The sick of the Naval Brigade had their immediate wants attended to by C. H. Barrett, Sickberth Steward of H.M.S. "Active," who, from his untiring exertions and unremitting attention to his duties, contracted fever himself, which nearly cost him his life. In case of alarm, a company of the crack shots of "the Buffs" was told off for manning the "loop-holes" in the hospital, and rough galleries were erected for the accommodation of these men; they were under the command of Capt. Gelston of that regiment.

The area of the fort inside the foot of the banquette was 69,200 square feet, that of the buildings 6100 square feet, so that the total available space for the men at night, exclusive of the sick within the church, was 63,100 square feet, allowing between three and four square yards per man. The daily ration was as follows:—coffee, $\frac{1}{3}$ oz.; tea, on three days in the week only, $\frac{1}{6}$ oz.; sugar, $1\frac{1}{4}$ oz.; salt, $\frac{1}{3}$ oz.; lime-juice, for a short period, $\frac{1}{2}$ oz.; compressed vegetables, for part of the time only, $\frac{1}{2}$ oz.; fresh meat (trek ox), $1\frac{1}{2}$ lbs.; bread-stuffs, either biscuit, Boers' meal, or mealie meal, $\frac{3}{4}$ lb. This was occasionally supplemented with pumpkin, or the young leaves of the white arum, boiled, which made an excellent dish, resembling spinach.

On Feb. 22nd, a sale by auction was held of articles found on turning out the contents of the waggons belonging to the volunteers

The Zulu War. 251

and other troops which had returned to the Lower Tugela. Some of the prices realized were—¼ lb. tobacco, 1*l.* 2*s.*; small bottle of curry powder, 1*l.* 7*s.*; tin of condensed milk, 1*l.*; bottle of pickles, 1*l.* 6*s.*; ½-pint bottle of sauce, 1*l.* 1*s.*; tin of salmon, 15*s.* 6*d.*; small tin of cocoa, 11*s.*; ham, weighing 12 lbs., 6*l.* 5*s.*

The drinking water at Ekowe was remarkably pure, and was pronounced by experienced men as some of the best in the Zulu country: the stream was always clear and running. A large swimming-bath was formed by widening and excavating the bed of this stream, in which, at proper hours, the men were permitted to bathe. At retreat every evening all the troops got under arms, and lined that part of the parapet which it was appointed to each corps to guard. To the Naval Brigade was entrusted the defence of the south-eastern side of the fort, and the sheen of the long line of cutlass bayonets in the moonlight presented a truly formidable appearance. In this part of the fort was the mission house, filled with the stores of the commissariat; the verandah forming the quarters of the officers of the Naval Brigade. Such vigilance was exercised after dark that the men who had periodically to inspect the safety of the cattle often ran great risks, and several times every night the call ran along the parapet from one guard to the next, "Sentry, there's a man gone out to look after the 'orses!" On one occasion a sentry was heard to challenge twice and then to fire into the darkness: a fusillade was immediately opened from all along the parapet, when it was discovered that the supposed enemy was a coat, which a man having washed during the afternoon had carelessly left hanging to dry on a stick. During the night, however, real Zulus were sometimes seen on the sky-lines of the adjacent hills. They would pull down the stakes which were placed to mark the distances, and cut down the small trees which they saw afforded shade to the videttes during the day: these were often fired at and sometimes wounded. One source of anxiety was the limited amount of ammunition in store; the original stock was about 340 rounds per man, but a good deal was expended in the frequent skirmishes which took place; and it was feared that, should the Zulu army be repulsed after a lengthened attack on the place, and it were subsequently to renew the assault, the ammunition would be exhausted. A quantity of loose powder and bullets had been left behind by the Natal Native Contingent. Case-shot for the guns was manufactured from the latter, by enclosing them in empty jam and other tins, and their efficiency tested by firing at groups of dummies placed to represent Zulus. The videttes used to amuse themselves by putting an old red coat and cap on a stick, so that in the distance it resembled a man: this device rarely failed to draw a fire from the Zulus, who were always lurking in the vicinity. As much as possible was done to enliven the garrison: the bands of "the Buffs" and of the 99th played on alternate days, and for several evenings Mr. Robertson gave interesting lectures on the history of the Zulus; we also had rubbers of whist in the afternoon, lawn tennis, quoits, and sometimes cricket. On Sundays there was always a church parade, generally in the early morning, and Moody and Sankey's hymn, "Hold the Fort," was for some time included in the service.

On March 1st, about 2 a.m., a column started to burn Xegwekane, a military kraal about six miles off, of which Dabulamanzi (so named from Dabula, "to cross through," Ama-nzi, "water," because, at the time of his birth, Panda crossed the Blood River—the

Zulus generally naming their children after some event which occurs about the period of their nativity), half brother of Ketchwayo, was the commander. This column consisted of the Royal Marines, H.M.S. "Active," company Royal Engineers, four companies "the Buffs," a company 99th, the Natal Native Pioneers, thirty mounted men, and a few Royal Artillery, with one gun, Col. Pearson taking the command. They groped their way in the dark, and when about three quarters of a mile distant from the kraal, and it was just getting light, some of the Zulus observed them, and a body of about fifty was immediately seen running to the kraal; several of these had red coats on, and consequently were not fired at, as it was thought they might possibly be some of the Natal Pioneers. Several kloofs had then to be passed through, and the occupants of the kraal, taken by surprise, were seen streaming up the hill beyond and urging forward their cattle. A shell was now fired into the kraal, which contained some forty or fifty huts, and then Lieut. Rowden, with the mounted infantry, rode forwards and set it on fire. A couple of shell were then fired among the retreating Zulus, and two were seen to fall; upon which Col.

Pearson, anxious to take a prisoner, so as to procure some information, ordered a force to hurry onwards and seize them. This proceeding, which proved futile, occupied a considerable time, during which the Zulus recovered from their panic and commenced to fire volleys from long distances, which were returned with shell; and as it was thought that they might do much harm by getting round and occupying the bush, a different route was chosen by which to return, and on the way three more kraals were burned, the Zulus still continuing to fire from a distance. No casualties occurred, and about 10 a.m. Ekowe was reached.

On March 2nd there was great excitement in the fort, as heliographic signals were seen coming from the direction of the Tugela; they appeared to proceed from a ridge between the Inyoni and St. Andrew's, and they were repeated several times, but nothing definite could be made out. Unsuccessful attempts were made to return them, every one who possessed anything in the shape of a mirror bringing it for trial, and, if visible, the number of flashes from different positions must have been very puzzling to the heliographers in the distance. This was the first communication we had received from the outer world since February 11th, and our anxiety as to the safety of the colony was very great. One day we saw numerous fires springing up across the Tugela, and a cry proceeded from one of the colonists, "The Zulus have got into Natal! Oh, my poor people!"—and it certainly looked as if kraals were being fired in all directions, and the attendant scenes of butchery were easily pictured. This probably arose from numerous grass fires lighted by the natives of Natal. The Zulus around Ekowe were constantly firing the grass on a large scale: it seemed at one time as if they were attempting to burn us out, or at least to destroy all the pasturage of our cattle. On the next day the signalling was repeated, and we made out what appeared to be, "Col. Law will advance as far as the Inyezane about the 13th, with a thousand men besides natives, to your relief; prepare to sally out and meet him with your surplus garrison." An attempt to communicate again was made the next day; but the Zulus fired the grass on the intervening country, which caused such a cloud of smoke as completely to obscure the flashes—whether this was done by accident or design was uncertain. The

The Zulu War.

same evening a body of some 3000 Zulus was observed about two miles away.

On the morning of the 5th the signalling was resumed, and the meaning of the preceding message verified.

It was now determined to make a road to join the main road to the Inyezane directly below Ekowe, and a strong reconnaissance having proceeded to examine the ground, Capt. Wynne pronounced it practicable, and, moreover, that it would effect a saving in distance of some five miles, the route through the Hintza Forest being entirely avoided. Parties now went to work with great zeal until this road was completed, but received much annoyance from the Zulus, who lined all the neighbouring ridges and crept up the valleys under cover of the high grass: skirmishes were of daily occurrence. One morning the enemy came on in such numbers that our men had to retire, although some very well directed shell were sent amongst the former; they resumed work, however, in the afternoon under the protection of a much stronger covering force. In one of these skirmishes Lieut. Lewis, of "the Buffs," was severely wounded in the forehead. The Engineers once placed a large charge of dynamite in the ground, surrounded it with heavy stones, drove in a stake to which an exploding apparatus was attached, and then retired. A number of Zulus proceeded to pull up the stake, when the dynamite exploded, killing and wounding several, and causing a terrible fright to the remainder; after this they seemed to keep at a more respectful distance. The heat was sometimes so great in the valleys through which this road passed, that several men who belonged to the working parties were brought in suffering from sunstroke.

March 10*th.*—A great deal of cheering was heard about 5.30 a.m., as a runner arrived, bringing a despatch a fortnight old, during which time he stated that he had been on the road: he wore a great coat belonging to a man of the 24th regiment. He informed us that he had been chased by the Zulus and was obliged to throw away his rifle, and that he had lived on mealies he had picked up in the fields. His story was so improbable, and appearances were so much against him, especially as he came in with his legs newly oiled and showed no signs of fatigue, that our natives wished to put him to death as a spy; but he was eventually made prisoner, and kept so by the Naval Brigade until our return to the Lower

Tugela: some shots were fired in the distance as he approached Ekowe, but this might have been an arranged thing.

The enemy throughout annoyed our videttes very much, and when they rode out the first thing of a morning to patrol the vicinity of the fort they often ran great risks; indeed, companies of infantry had frequently to clear the surrounding hills before they could be posted. A private of the 99th, called Kent, belonging to the mounted infantry, was killed by an ambuscade of Zulus: his horse galloped to the fort covered with blood. A party was immediately despatched to make a search, and found the body lying in the grass, with eighteen assegai wounds in it, the man's rifle and ammunition having been taken away. Another vidette, called Carson, also of the 99th, was riding along a ridge when some twenty Zulus immediately sprang up, fired a volley at about twelve yards distance, and then, rushing on, assegaied the horse: this man, however, managed to get away and gallop to the fort, where he was found to have been severely wounded by bullets in five places.

On the 12th March we despatched a runner to the Tugela, by a circuitous route, with the information that we could make our provisions last till April 7th, as we had been asked the question by heliograph. The next day the so-called surplus garrison, consisting of the same force before mentioned as about to proceed to the Lower Tugela, had made every preparation for marching; but we were informed by heliograph " that the advance of Col. Law's column was cancelled, and that a force consisting of 4000 white troops and 2000 natives would leave the Tugela for Ekowe on April 1st; that the 60th Rifles were to replace us here, and that we were to return, with all our empty waggons; that 8000 troops, in fifteen transports, were on their way from England; and that the 57th regt. had already landed; and also that the runners, whom we had despatched yesterday, had arrived." Large bodies of Zulus, many thousands in number, had been seen from the Observatory Hill for two or three days, coming from the interior, and moving towards the Inyezane. They had evidently got some intelligence of the advance of Col. Law's column, so that, had we marched, both forces, while trying to effect a junction, would probably have suffered heavily. Heliographic signalling was now carried on daily whenever the weather permitted, and the messages were very care-

The Zulu War.

fully read by one of the signalmen of the Naval Brigade and by a corporal of "the Buffs;" the news received during the day always being posted on a notice-board inside the fort. Rockets were sometimes fired at the Tugela after dark, which we returned. An attempt was made by the Engineers to send back messages by means of a large movable black screen placed on the top of a hill, so that it should show against the sky, but unsuccessfully; subsequently, however, a large mirror was fixed in position, and the long and short flashes made by covering it temporarily with a hand-board, which answered completely.

On the 15th March an immense array of Zulus, calculated by experienced observers at 20,000 men, was seen moving away from the noighbourhood of the Inyezane and returning up country: they had doubtless discovered that our arrangements for the 13th had been altered. The heliograph informed us "that the 91st Highlanders had arrived at the Cape; that Commodore Sullivan had been made an Admiral; and that 300 Shahs were at the Tugela." As we knew that H.M.S. "Shah" was not in this part of the world, it was supposed that the word should have been read "Sikhs," and that some of these troops had been sent from India; we were, however, enlightened by succeeding communications.

On the 16th we lost one of our mess. Mr. Coker, midshipman, died of dysentery, with which he had been ill for some weeks: it was induced by sleeping at night in the open, at his post beside the Gatling gun, during very wet weather. He was of a most genial, kindly disposition, and gave great promise of being an excellent officer. He was buried on the following day, and being generally beloved, nearly every officer in the fort followed his remains to the grave, Capt. Campbell and myself being the chief mourners. The cemetery at Ekowe was a pattern of neatness and good taste. Capt. Gelston, of "the Buffs," devoted a great part of his time to it. At the head of nearly every grave was a nicely finished Latin cross, or a modification of that emblem, made generally of wood: the inscriptions were cleverly carved, several of them by Gelston himself and by Dr. Giles, one of the medical officers. Many were the hours passed by the former in this labour of love, and in manufacturing articles of furniture and other things which contributed materially to the comfort of the poor sufferers in the hospital. Flowers, ferns, and small shrubs were planted about this cemetery, the graves were neatly turfed, and the whole was enclosed by light wooden railings. When we evacuated the fort we left behind us, in this "God's acre," Mr. Coker, midshipman; J. Moore, shoemaker; J. Radford, leading seaman; W. Stagg, private R.M.L.I.; and A. Smith, able seaman, all belonging to the Naval Brigade. Their graves received the constant care of the men, and especially that of Mr. Coker, who was a general favourite among them; they erected a cross at his head, on which was neatly carved by one of them the following inscription—" In Memory of Lewis Cadwallader Coker, Midshipman, Naval Brigade, H.M.S. 'Active,' who died at Ekowe, March 16th, 1879, aged 19 years." There was also carved in relief a broken anchor within a circle. There were likewise buried here Capt. H. J. Williams and Lieut. G. R. Evelyn, of "the Buffs," and Lieut. A. S. Davidson, of the 99th, with eight men of the former and eight of the latter regiment, and one man of the Army Hospital Corps. The bodies of two or three men who died soon after our arrival at Ekowe were interred in other places. The heliograph informed us that "Admiral Sullivan had turned over the naval command of the station to Commodore Richards, and that the 'Active' had left Durban." On the 23rd it was flashed to us that "Ketchwayo, being in despair with regard to dislodging us, was about to try and draw us out of the fort." The same afternoon two Zulus were seen in the distance waving a white flag. Several officers rode out to ascertain who they were: they were closely questioned through Mr. Robertson, then blindfolded, brought to the fort, and put in irons. The story of one man was that he had been sent by Ketchwayo to Bishop Schroeder at Kranzkop, to inquire why we were making war upon him, as we had always objected to his fighting with other nations. The answer he received was that we were merely carrying out the terms of the Tugela *ultimatum;* and that the king had now sent him there to say that he had no wish to injure us, and that if we would promise not to destroy the mealie fields and gardens, we had his full permission to march to the Tugela unmolested. The other man stated that he had been ordered by Dabulamanzi to accompany the first, and that, should we agree to the king's terms, he was to instruct the commanders of the Impis which were surrounding Ekowe that they were to let us pass. It would have been unnecessary to state that both these wily men were kept close prisoners, had it not appeared that some people in England professed to be highly indignant because "Ketchwayo's two peaceful ambassadors to Ekowe had been put in irons." Such persons must either have been lamentably ignorant of Zulu antecedents, or must have imagined, what it is difficult to comprehend, viz., that the affairs of their countrymen can be dealt with much better by people several thousand miles away than they can possibly be by those on the spot, acquainted with the circumstances of a case, for I presume that they are too generous not to accord that humanity to their countrymen which they claim for themselves. Had these men escaped, after providing themselves with every information about the fort, the consequence it is difficult to foresee. Mr. Robertson elicited from them that the total strength of their army around Ekowe was about 30,000, but this was probably an exaggerated statement. Still there must have been a very large force, as towards sunset we could see the lines of smoke from their cooking fires rising from behind every ridge between us and the Inyezane.

On the 29th two brave men of the Natal Native Pioneers, whom, at my request, Mr. Robertson had induced to go to the Lower Tugela for medicines, returned with several valuable drugs, also two English newspapers. A sum of money was raised by subscription, and presented to them. They stated that the neighbourhood of the Tugela was covered with troops, which were just on the eve of advancing, and that the Natal Zulus had informed some of their kinsmen who lived in the Zulu country of the impending march, by calling across the river, in their figurative style, "The cow is just going to calve." The physical condition of the garrison was getting much reduced, and the men could not resist disease as they formerly did: upwards of a hundred sick were sometimes seen by the medical officers of a morning. We were told by signal yesterday that the relieving force, under Lord Chelmsford, would probably leave the Tugela to-day or to-morrow; and in the evening we saw watch-fires near the Inyoni, probably those of that force, as no Zulus would encamp in such an open place so near the Tugela.

April 2*nd*.—For the past two nights we had observed fires gradually nearing us, along the neighbourhood known as the coast, or John Dunn's road, and we saw by day, much to our delight, the cavalry of the relieving column scouring the low country between us and the Amatakulu, and firing the kraals in all directions. Yesterday evening we noticed that the force had laagered between the Amatakulu and the Inyezane, near the site of the military kraal of Ginginlhovo, which we had burned on our march to Ekowe. This morning, about 6 a.m., we heard the distant booming of guns. Many of us immediately repaired to an eminence nearly 500 yards from the fort, and at some ten miles distance below us we descried the Zulu army engaged in a general attack on the laager of our relieving force: the dark bodies of Zulus and the line of waggons could just be distinguished by the naked eye, but with a good telescope the whole action might be plainly seen. We could also hear indistinctly the reports of the rifles, but those of the Gatling guns of the Naval Brigade were very audible. The Zulus appeared to advance very determinedly, and the battle raged for about an hour; and shortly after 7 a.m. they were observed to have retreated generally, desultory firing only going on in the foreground from some troops which had evidently left the laager to harass the retreating enemy. When the Zulu prisoner, whom we captured after our engagement at Inyezane, heard the noise of the distant battle, he burst into tears, which flowed nearly the whole time. After the action the General flashed to us that "he would advance to-morrow to our relief with three regiments, and hoped to reach us the same evening; that Ekowe was to be altogether abandoned, it being situated in so inaccessible a country; that in future the coast road to Ulundi would be the one adopted; all material which it was not possible to take away was to be destroyed; and a fort would be constructed somewhere near his present position." We received the news that Ekowe was to be permanently abandoned with regret, as we had laboured hard to improve it in every way, and it was now a most perfect fortress, notwithstanding its bad position. We received from the Tugela by signal the news of Col. Wood's victory at Kambula. In the afternoon we saw long lines of the defeated Zulus treking away northwards along the coast country. They halted for some time at a large kraal towards the Umlalazi River, and then appeared to separate and take different routes. We also observed parties busily at work on the ground surrounding Lord Chelmsford's laager. We concluded, and rightly, that they were burying the slain. The following is the account which I received from one who was present in this battle, which is known as that of Ginginlhovo:—"Towards 6 a.m. our patrols, which had been sent out some time before, came in with the news that they had to retire, as large bodies of the enemy were advancing from the direction of the Inyezane. These were also observed from the laager." I may mention that a laager consists of an enclosure formed by waggons placed closely but somewhat obliquely together; at some distance outside them a shelter trench is dug; the defenders occupy the space between the trench and the waggons, and the former itself in case of necessity. The area enclosed by the waggons contains all the cattle. In the present instance the laager was about 130 yards square; its front was towards the Inyezane and the Ekowe heights, its rear faced the distant sea, its left was opposite the Amatakulu Bush, and its right looked towards the charred remains of the military kraal of Ginginlhovo. "Every preparation was at once made to give them a fitting reception. The defenders of the laager consisted of the Naval Brigade, represented by the contingents of H.M. ships 'Boadicea,' 'Shah,' and 'Tenedos,' with four 24-pounder rocket-tubes, two Gatlings, and two 9-pounder guns, under Commander Brackenbury, R.N., the Marines being commanded by Capt. Philips, R.M.L.I., both of H.M.S. 'Shah;' the 57th, 3rd battalion 60th, 91st, several companies of the 2nd battalion 'the Buffs,' and of the 99th regiment; Mounted Infantry, Natal Volunteer Horse, and Mounted Basutos; two battalions Natal Native Contingent; and Mr. John Dunn, with 150 of his men, known as 'Dunn's Scouts;' the total strength being about 3400 Europeans and 2500 natives. Lieut. Milne, of H.M.S. 'Active,' was with Lord Chelmsford as Naval A.D.C., and Capt. Richards, R.N., the new commodore of the station, also accompanied the column. The four angles of the square and the adjacent parts of each front were defended by the Naval Brigade, with its artillery; the infantry lined each face of the laager; while the cavalry and native regiments were behind these; the tops of the waggons being occupied by conductors and others who possessed fire-arms, and among them was Mr. Dunn, who is celebrated as a marksman, and did much execution from this elevated position. The Zulu plan of attack was the usual and traditional one, viz. that of surrounding their enemy. Their columns advanced from three different directions—the two stronger from the Inyezane, the two weaker, one from the direction of the burnt kraal, the other from the Amatakulu Bush. From the two stronger columns the usual horns were sent out, which extended as rapidly as possible, so as to try and encircle the laager; the Naval Brigade having the honour of commencing the engagement with its artillery. The enemy, opening a heavy fire, continued to advance, amid perfect silence and with the greatest courage, and even came within some twenty or thirty yards of one of the Gatling guns. The grass being very high, the Zulus derived great advantage in the way of cover, and they doggedly maintained their ground for some time, although falling rapidly, making several desperate attempts to carry the lines; but were received with so hot a fire, that probably no troops in the world would have stood before it. They first began to retreat from that side of the laager which looked towards the sea: then Major Barrow and his cavalry executed a rapid charge with their sabres, killing upwards of a hundred of the enemy. The Natal Native Contingent now rushed out on the wavering masses of Zulus, which, having fired into them, took to flight; this flight soon became general on all sides, a storm of shot being sent after the fugitives. The reserves on the hills also retired, but in good order. A large body of the beaten Zulus collected on a hill about a mile away, and became a good mark for the gunners of the Naval Brigade, whose shell were so accurately pitched by these gunners, under Lieut. C. Lindsay, R.N., that several Zulus were killed, and the remainder soon disappeared. Lord Chelmsford, attired in a red night-cap, was seen everywhere along the faces of the laager on foot, giving directions. The cool behaviour of the Naval Brigade was pronounced as splendid, and the men appeared much disappointed that the affair was over so soon. The wounded of the Naval Brigade in this action consisted of Lieut. Milne and one seaman, H.M.S. 'Active;' two seamen and one marine, 'Boadicea;' two seamen, 'Shah;' and Staff-Surgeon W. Longfield, 'Tenedos,' who was dangerously wounded in the arm and chest. They were well attended to by Staff-Surgeon Shields and Surgeon Sibbald of the 'Shah,' and Surgeon Pollard of the 'Boadicea.' The enemy numbered about 12,000 men, who were under the command of the Induna Somapo and of Dabulamanzi, and his loss in killed was probably 1200." The Zulus had no idea of the large number of troops in the laager, but imagined that there could not be sufficient to defend it on all sides at once, and that by surrounding it they would be sure to get in somewhere.

On the morning of April 3rd the following was flashed to us from the laager:—" The three regiments started from here for Ekowe about 8 a.m. Result of General's engagement yesterday:—Lieut. Johnson, 99th, and 3 men killed; Col. Northey, 60th, Staff-Surgeon Longfield, R.N., Capt. Hinchman, 57th, and 25 men wounded. 470 Zulus buried close round the laager."

At 4 p.m., Col. Pearson, with 500 of the garrison, left Ekowe, to meet the General and our relieving force; they took the new road and returned about 6 p.m. The first arrival at Ekowe was that of Capt. Newman, a newspaper correspondent, who gave us all the news of the past two months, and at the same time, with professional aptitude, took in all that he could of our doings during the same period. It was a beautiful moonlight night, and about 7.15 a tremendous "hurrah" from all along the parapet announced the arrival of Lord Chelmsford and the head of his column, and that Ekowe was relieved. As the 91st Highlanders marched up the valley, their pipers struck up "The Campbells are coming," which was to most of us the sweetest music we ever heard. The troops, as they arrived, bivouacked on the hill on the further side of the stream from which we procured our water; the last of them did not reach Ekowe till midnight. The relieving force consisted of a company of marines under Capt. Philips, R.M.L.I., a company of blue-jackets under Lieut. Carr, R.N., a squadron of horse, the 57th, 60th, and 91st regiments, and Mr. Dunn, with his scouts. Commodore Richards also accompanied the General, as did likewise Lieut. Milne, Naval A.D.C. to Lord Chelmsford; and very glad we all were to shake hands with our gallant young messmate again. He brought us two bags of mails, and the avidity with which the letters were torn open, and their contents devoured, surpasses description.

April 4*th*.—All our waggons were in perfect readiness to move, and 400 fully-equipped trek oxen, which were signalled for yesterday, arrived from the laager to draw them. I had twelve ambulances and waggons fitted up for the worst cases of sickness, and fortunate it was that we were relieved, for only a very few days' rations remained, and many of the garrison were in a most feeble condition; Capt. Wynne and Lieut. Willock, of the Royal Engineers, and Lieut. Thirkill, 88th, being especially in a critical state, as also were many of the men, more particularly those of the 99th regt. Lord Chelmsford and Commodore Richards went through the hospital, and appeared to take a warm interest in the sick; and on my informing them of the general condition of the garrison, it was decided that the men should remain for a short time at Fort Pearson to recruit. The former afterwards started with the cavalry and Dunn's scouts to burn Dabulamanzi's private kraal. At 1 p.m. the garrison of Ekowe set out for the Lower Tugela, by the old road through the Hintza Forest, with 119 waggons. We saw in front of us a dense column of smoke, which arose from Dabulamanzi's kraal, which was now in flames, and we observed the General's force returning in the distance. We heard that a few Zulus had fired on our people at long ranges, and that Dabulamanzi was present on horseback, but that he quickly dismounted on discovering the perfection of John Dunn's rifle practice. It was a delightful sensation being free once more after so close an incarceration. We laagered about 5 p.m. on exactly the same spot on which we bivouacked after the battle of Inyezane.

About eight o'clock the next morning we left the laager, having been joined by a troop of mounted Basutos, under Capt. Hay, and at the same time the advanced guard of Lord Chelmsford's column was seen descending from Ekowe by the new road. As we proceeded, we passed the waggons which had been abandoned by the convoy under Lieut.-Col. Eley: the linch-pins had been all removed, and the smell from the decomposing stores, which lay scattered about, was sickening. Further on we passed an extensive bush in a valley, where a large Zulu force had evidently been lying for a long period, and it was some of the smoke from their fires curling above the ridges which we used to observe from Ekowe of an evening. Still further on we found that the road, as it ran round the side of a steep hill, had been cut away by the Zulus, so as to stop the progress of our waggons had we attempted to evacuate Ekowe: this had been repaired by the relieving force on its way up. About a mile beyond this we crossed the site of our old battle-field of January 22nd. We paused to examine it, and, considering the great strength of the positions held by the enemy, we congratulated ourselves that we had defeated him with so little loss. We found the grave of our slain untouched; the cross remained, but Capt. Gelston now replaced it with a much larger and more handsome one, which had cost him several days' labour. The Naval Brigade was in advance to-day, and a very hot wearisome trek we had; the men marched well on the whole, but many were unable to continue it long from weakness, and there were one or two cases of sunstroke. While we were on the march we received orders to return to the Tugela by our old route through the Amatakulu Bush, as this was shorter than that by the coast road. A large number of kraals were burnt by the way, principally by the Basutos, who scoured all the adjacent districts on their nimble little horses, and hundreds of huts were shortly in flames. The ancient Zulu dame, who was found on the day that we destroyed the Ginginlhovo military kraal, and whom Mr. Robertson had taken charge of, returned with us. She had remained in Ekowe ever since, where she was known as "Old Nanny," and it was a matutinal amusement with the blue-jackets to lend her a pannican of water and then stand round to see her wash. We laagered in the afternoon on the outskirts of the Amatakulu Bush, close to the spot where we had encamped on the evening of January 21st. Near us was the place where one corps of the Zulu army, which had attacked Lord Chelmsford at Ginginlhovo three days before, had lain on the night previous: beneath every bush there had been a fire, and round them a circle of Zulus had slept, while the long grass was everywhere trampled down, proving that a considerable force had been present. One tree, which had drooping branches, had been covered over with long grass, so as to form a kind of hut, and this had probably been occupied by the principal

Indunas. This Impi had left a large number of things behind, or they might have been thrown away by the fugitives after the battle—assegai sheaths, mats, armlets, and pieces of rug, and there was also the corpse of a Zulu, with a severe bullet-wound in the abdomen. This man had probably been wounded at Ginginlhovo, and had reached thus far before he fell. A couple of our officers rode to the General's laager, which was about three miles off. When they returned they stated that the air was tainted with the number of corpses which they had passed.

We quitted our laager at 7 a.m. on the 6th, passed through the thick Amatakulu Bush, and forded that river. Shortly after noon we outspanned on the left bank of the Umsundusi and "parked" our waggons, to permit the rear of the column to come up, which was formed to-day of the Naval Brigade and the 99th, as Col. Pearson had received information that two Zulu Impis had been seen on our right towards Kranzkop: these, however, were probably the remains of some of the shattered corps from Ginginlhovo. Whilst here we were joined by Lieut. Abbott, R.N., of H.M.S. "Shah," and Mr. Myers, a newspaper correspondent, who had ridden from the Lower Tugela to meet us. Some of the sick were rapidly succumbing : two young soldiers of the 99th died to-day, and many were getting extremely feeble, among whom were Capt. Wynne, R.E., and Lieut. Thirkill, 88th, before mentioned, who both died within a short time of our reaching the Tugela. We continued our march about 5 p.m., and during a beautifully clear moonlight night; crossed the Inyoni about 9 p.m., and at midnight bivouacked about a mile from St. Andrew's mission station; it was, however, 3 a.m. before the rear of the column came in. We discarded tents on the march down, except for the sick.

April 7th.—Inspanned at 8 a.m., and at 11 a.m. arrived once more on the banks of the Lower Tugela, where we were received most enthusiastically by the troops encamped there. We crossed the river on the pont, and during the evening the contingent to the Naval Brigade from H.M.S. "Active" encamped on the Euphorbia Hill, a magnificent site not far from Fort Pearson, which was also occupied by a company of our men. At the time of our arrival Ford Tenedos was held by a body of men from H.M. ships

The Zulu War.

"Boadicea" and "Shah." Both the forts had undergone considerable alterations since we left: they were now surrounded by iron gabions filled with earth; a shelter trench likewise extended from Fort Pearson to the foot of Euphorbia Hill, on the summit of which was also an earthwork.

The Naval Brigade at this time in the field consisted of forty-one officers and 812 men, thus constituted:—

	Offs.	Men.	
H.M.S. "Active".	10	158	landed Nov. 19, 1878.
„ "Boadicea".	10	218	„ Mar. 18, 1879.
„ "Flora."	2	0	„ April 20, „
„ "Shah."	16	378	„ Mar. 7, „
„ "Tenedos".	3	58	„ Jan. 1, „
	41	812	

Capt H. F. Campbell, of H.M.S. "Active," was in command of the entire brigade, with Lieut. Craigie, of the same ship, as Staff-officer. The contingent of H.M.S. "Active" was commanded by Lieut. Hamilton; that of the "Boadicea" by Commander Romilly; "Shah," Commander Brackenbury; and "Tenedos," Lieut. Kingscote. On May 2nd this latter contingent was withdrawn, and left for Durban, to rejoin the ship.

Until June 17th, the date of our second advance into the Zulu country, the Naval Brigade was divided into two principal parts, one of which was stationed at the Lower Tugela, occupying Forts Pearson and Tenedos; the other at Fort Chelmsford, a new stronghold, which had been formed beyond Ginginlhovo, on the banks of the Inyezane, and which was designed to fulfil the same purpose for which Ekowe was originally intended, viz., as an advanced post at which stores might be accumulated. Large numbers of well-filled waggons, accompanied by strong convoys, were constantly passing from the Lower Tugela to this fort, a distance of some twenty-five miles, and returning empty, unless occupied by sick men, as the situation proved to be very unhealthy.

The Natal Kafirs were evidently very much impressed with the number of soldiers they saw landing in the country; the force at the Tugela alone drew from many of them expressions of astonishment—they had no idea that we could bring such numbers into the field. One man was heard to exclaim, "The Zulus have been kicking the Ant Hill too hard at last, and the ants are beginning to pour out." Major-General Crealock arrived at the Lower Tugela, and took the command of the forces which collectively were to constitute the first division of the army in Zululand. Maquenda, one of Ketchwayo's half-brothers, came in and surrendered, with a few of his people, and they were placed under the surveillance of Mr. Fynney, the Border Agent. During my stay at the Tugela on this occasion I made the acquaintance of the Rev. Mr. Oftebro, who was formerly the occupant of the mission station at Ekowe, and who was residing in the neighbourhood with his family; he informed me that the buildings at Ekowe were entirely erected and finished by his nephew and himself, and that they had even made the bricks. His nephew was a medical man, and had been Ketchwayo's medical adviser. Our sojourn at the Tugela greatly improved the physique of the "Actives," and when we again advanced into the Zulu country, on June 17th, they had regained their pristine condition.

At noon on this day the following force left the Lower Tugela, under Gen. Crealock, with upwards of a hundred carts and waggons:—Part of the Naval Brigade, with one 9-pounder and three Gatling guns, a few Royal Artillery and Royal Engineers, 88th regiment, a part of the third battalion 60th Rifles, and the 57th regiment. We left behind us Mr. Cotter, our boatswain, in command of a party of blue-jackets as a garrison for Fort Tenedos. Before reaching St. Andrew's we took a road to the right, known as the coast route, or John Dunn's road : its advantage being that it passed through an open country almost entirely free from bush; its disadvantages, that it was much more unhealthy than the old road by Ekowe, and the distance to Ulundi farther. About 3 p.m. we reached a large entrenched place on the top of a hill known as "Walker's Laager." The interior of this, like that of all the other laagers on the route, had been occupied by every convoy which had passed to and fro between the Tugela and Fort Chelmsford for more than two months, and the result was that all had become extremely foul; and the neighbouring streams, from which the drinking-water was obtained, was too often tainted by the decomposing carcasses of oxen, which, abandoned on the road, had just strength enough remaining to crawl there to drink, and then died. At Fort Chelmsford these conditions culminated, for here the remains of Zulus as well as of oxen were taken out of the Inyezane, the water of which the garrison had been drinking for some time. Not far from this "Walker's Laager" was the late residence of Mr. John Dunn; and while our food was being cooked, Dr. Grant, R.N., and myself, walked over to inspect it. It consisted of several detached one-storied houses, built of corrugated iron, with wooden floors: the principal house contained eight small rooms; the windows, which had been glazed, had all been broken. Near these houses was a large cattle kraal encircled by Zulu huts: the whole was situated on the slope of a hill, a stream surrounding it on three sides. The nights were very cold at this time of the year, and I envied Grant his warm Scotch plaid, in which he enveloped himself before going to sleep.

I was awoke early the next morning by hearing a man, who was sleeping beneath a waggon near me, exclaim that "his nose was froze on to the cart wheel." The reveillé was sounded at 6 a.m., whilst it was quite dark, and we started on our march at seven o'clock; shortly after which the sun rose, and it soon became correspondingly hot. The road was very dusty, and we frequently passed the swollen carcasses of bullocks, which exhaled a horrible odour. About 4 p.m. we crossed the Amatakulu River, near the further bank of which, constructed on a commanding site, and surrounded to a great extent by the river, which here made a remarkable curve, was Fort Crealock, which served to protect the route to Fort Chelmsford, and that too at a very important point: it was held by a couple of companies of "the Buffs:" and in a most foul but delightfully situated laager beyond this, just above the spot where the Inyezane joins the Amatakulu, we spent the night. The two companies of "the Buffs" now joined our division, having been relieved by part of the 88th regiment; but we could not start from our laager until 11 a.m., as it was necessary to allow time for the oxen to graze. At 4 p.m. we reached Fort Chelmsford, which was placed in a most unexceptionable position from a military point of view, but in a very unhealthy locality. We crossed the Inyezane, and encamped on a hill about half a mile beyond. Here we were joined by the remainder of the Naval Brigade, under Commander Brackenbury. At 9 a.m. the next day a force consisting of the greater portion of the Naval Brigade, with its artillery, under Capt. Campbell; "the Buffs," the Natal Native Contingent, and Dunn's scouts, paraded on the plain, and then marched for the

Umlalazi River. The Natal native regiment was now completely clothed in scarlet tunics, and was armed throughout with Martini-Henry rifles, which made them very proud, and imbued them with immense confidence. We passed along an open but boggy country: it must have been sparsely inhabited, judging from the very few sites of kraals which we passed; the kraals themselves had been all fired above a month before by Major Barrow and his cavalry. We reached the right bank of the Umlalazi without encountering any opposition, and formed an entrenched camp in a well-selected position, the naval gun having first shelled a bush on the opposite bank to dislodge any of the enemy which might be lurking there, and a large kraal just beyond was set on fire. From this camp we enjoyed a capital view of the Observatory Hill at Ekowe, and from thence a range extended away to the eastward, covered for a long distance by a forest known as the Ungoya, which was only a few miles away; and here Mr. Dunn had a large estate. Our camp was afterwards reinforced by the 91st Highlanders, under Col. Bruce. On the morning of the 22nd a pontoon bridge was constructed across the river, and an earthwork was commenced on a hill on the further side, to protect the bridge, and serve to keep open the communication for a further advance: this was named Fort Napoleon, in remembrance of the young Prince Imperial of France, who had been so unfortunately killed a short time before. Here we left ten seamen gunners, with a gun, as part of the garrison. Dunn's scouts and part of the Natal native regiment, having crossed the bridge, soon spread all over the adjacent country, plundering and burning kraals. I met a party of our native servants from Natal hurrying away to join these, armed with guns and axes. On asking them where they were going, one fellow said, "Me shoot Zulu with gun, and then me chop him up with axe;" another remarked, "All the Zulus in Ungoya Forest up there, me see their fires last night—when you go to forest they all run away other side;" "Ah, cowards!" apostrophized a third. As it was difficult to remember the Kafir names of these men, we called them after certain insects with which we were constantly pestered, and they answered to the names of Tick, Spider, Flea, Fly, and Beetle. Gen. Crealock and Commodore Richards joined this camp, also a large body of cavalry, consisting of Lonsdale's

Horse, Natal Volunteer Horse, and mounted infantry, under Major Barrow; likewise the 60th Rifles and the 57th regiment. The cavalry, with a party of Dunn's scouts, made reconnaissance beyond the Umlalazi, having gone for several miles. When they returned, in the evening, they brought in about 160 Zulus, of both sexes, who had given themselves up, together with 150 head of splendid cattle; these latter had probably never seen either a white face or a red coat before—they were exceedingly wild and frightened : the Zulus were quartered in a kraal just beyond the river. On June 24th a strong patrol of cavalry and infantry left to try and find a road to a spot on the beach, which Lieut. Sidney Smith, R.N., commanding the gunboat " Forester," had discovered as a place where a landing might probably be effected. This was erroneously called Port Durnford, a name which many years before had been applied, without any substantial reason, to the mouth of the Umlalazi. This patrol was partly successful in discovering a route, and brought back about fifty head of cattle. On the 25th, the 88th regiment arrived from Fort Chelmsford. The Naval Brigade in this camp now consisted of twenty-one officers and 514 men

Gen. Crealock's division furnishing a total of 4488 European troops and 780 natives. We heard that all the Zulus in the neighbourhood had retired, with their cattle, beyond the Umslatoosi.

On the 26th a somewhat corpulent Induna, called Usintwangu, arrived as an ambassador from Ketchwayo, bearing an enormous tusk of ivory, which denotes a desire for peace, also a dozen fine cattle. Our cavalry started in the morning and scoured the hill-country towards Ekowe and the Ungoya, capturing a large herd of cattle and setting on fire an immense number of kraals: I counted twenty-one kraals burning at one time. A few Zulus, who showed armed opposition, were killed. At 1 p.m. the Naval Brigade and "the Buffs" marched out of the camp and crossed the Umlalazi, *en route* for the so-called Port Durnford, the division having been now separated into two brigades, Col. Rowlands, V.C., taking command of the 1st brigade, of which the naval forces formed part. After going a short distance we passed a large kraal on the summit of a low hill: from its situation I judged this to be the one at which the discomfited Zulu Impi halted after the Battle of Ginginlhovo,

The Zulu War.

as we observed from Ekowe. It was occupied at present by about 40 Zulu men, and 150 women and children, who had surrendered. The cavalry joined us at our next laager and preceded us on the march, and soon the smoke ascended from a score of burning kraals. We were obliged to halt for some time whilst a road was made across a swamp; this was quickly accomplished by laying down branches lopped from the trees in a forest close at hand, and then covering them with sods. We afterwards had to cut a road through part of this forest, in which grew magnificent cotton-trees, having huge ferns hanging from their trunks. The country we traversed subsequently contained numerous palm-trees, bearing a large dry-looking fruit, somewhat resembling a pear, which grew in clusters, and had in the interior a white kernel resembling ivory. We laagered about 4 p.m., on the top of a chain of hills, which was covered with the sweet-potato plant, on the tubers of which our men made a hearty meal. Immediately below us was a picturesque fresh-water lake, where the papyrus grew luxuriantly, and at no great distance was the Umlalazi, flowing into the sea. All along the coast was a low-lying swamp, with a sandy ridge between it and the sea, covered with trees. I noticed here among our Natal native troops some of the Amabomvu tribe, which resides near the Umzimkulu River. The people of this tribe have a curious custom of amputating the last phalanx of the little finger of the left hand when children, which is the distinguishing mark of that tribe. Our road the next day extended along the top of the ridge, where we passed one or two partially burned kraals: in one of the huts which remained were two very old women, wrinkled hags, with short white wool on their heads, and skins like brown parchment. One was asked why she remained, and had not departed with her children: she replied, "I am not a woman at all now, I am only a spirit." I was informed that they always look on themselves in this manner, when they become extremely old. We afterwards crossed an extensive, rather marshy plain, thinly covered with short rush; not a kraal was to be seen on it, except in one or two situations, where there was a low hill; and I noticed, in passing through this country, how, by a passive experience—I might, perhaps, call it instinct—these people, utterly ignorant of all sanitary matters, build their kraals in none but the most healthy situations. We at length encamped on the most distant part of this plain, in company with "the Buffs" and the 88th regt., which formed the 1st brigade. Our camp was quadrangular, and was soon surrounded by a well-made shelter-trench and low earthwork. Gen. Crealock, with the remainder of his force, which constituted the 2nd brigade, occupied another camp, at a distance of about half a mile; while the native troops formed a third and distinct camp. We were about three-quarters of a mile from the sea, which was approached by passing downwards between two ridges, the one on the left thinly covered with palm-trees, that on the right by thick forest; and through this gorge two streams, which flowed by our camps, united to reach the sea. A little to the left of this point, on the open sandy beach, was the spot newly named Port Durnford. We remained in this camp for more than three weeks, daily expecting an order, which, to our intense chagrin, never arrived, viz., to march on Ulundi, which was only some seventy miles distant. Wood was cut down, the stream bridged, and a very fair road made from the camp to the sea; and a quadrangular earthwork was thrown up, to serve as a fort, which, however, was never completed, owing to the sandy nature of the soil. We saw in different parts of this neighbourhood tokens of the visit of H.M.S. "Forester," in the shape of large conical shot; it appeared that her boats had been fired on by the Zulus when taking soundings, upon which she had opened fire on them with her heavy guns.

On the 30th June, two large steamers laden with stores arrived, together with the "Forester." It was a day of great interest to the Naval Brigade. Most of the men were ordered to the beach, where they worked with a will, the commodore superintending; and after the hawsers had been brought on shore and made fast, 18 tons of stores were at once landed, in a lighter, to the intense astonishment of the Kafir spectators, who were heard to exclaim, "Ah! Ketchwayo was a fool to fight the English;" and to the great credit of Lieut. Sidney Smith, the discoverer of this landing-place, which, could it have been utilized earlier, would have imparted new life to the whole campaign, as it saved a hundred miles of transport. This landing-place was on the open beach, without any shelter whatever; but the surf, for some

The Zulu War.

reason, was much less at this point than at any other along the coast. Maquenda, Ketchwayo's half-brother, who was with us, expressed the greatest surprise at the sight of a ship, which he had never before beheld, except on the horizon. After this the landing, which was a complete success, went on regularly, whenever the surf permitted, until very large stores of provisions, forage, ammunition, horses, mules, and all military necessaries were put on shore; these operations being conducted by two naval transport officers, Commander E. H. Davis, late of H.M.S. "Active," and Lieut. C. Caffin.

On July 2nd, H.M.S. "Shah" arrived, with General Sir Garnet Wolseley on board. A heavy south-westerly gale came on, which continued until the 5th, and all the ships had to put to sea. The "Shah" returned to Durban, Sir G. Wolseley being in despair about landing after his detention on board. On the 3rd, 250 of our cavalry, with John Dunn's scouts, burnt Emangwene, a very large military kraal several miles away, and captured some 600 cattle. News arrived on the 4th that Lord Chelmsford had been victorious in a great battle at Ulundi, and had burned the royal kraal. Numerous

Zulus came in and surrendered, and were permitted to reside in the bush, between the camp of the Natal native regiment and the sea.

On the 5th there was a grand parade of all the division, to receive the surrender of a body of some 600 Zulus, about 240 of whom were men; they brought with them 53 guns, and a large number of assegais. Our troops formed a long double line across the plain, the Naval Brigade taking the right—in front was the General and staff. Five old chiefs came forward, attired in long, many-coloured gowns; around them were the ring-headed men, and in bodies on either side were the younger men; behind stood the women and children, and still more posteriorly were all their cattle. Gen. Crealock addressed them through an interpreter, saying that, "if he allowed them to surrender, they must conform to the rules which he laid down; that they had fought well for their king and country, and were brave men; but that they were now thoroughly beaten, and were subjects of the Queen of England, and would have to give up Ketchwayo; that they would be provided with 'passes,' to show that they had surrendered; and he hoped that, for the future, the English and themselves would live on friendly terms." At the conclusion of each sentence the chiefs all exclaimed, "Ah! Inkos," and the speech seemed to satisfy them very much. They were manifestly astonished at the great display of troops, especially when the long lines presented arms; but what excited their curiosity most was the sound of the drums and bagpipes of the 91st Highlanders as that regiment marched away.

On the 6th the news of Lord Chelmsford's victory at Ulundi was confirmed, and twenty-one guns were fired in honour of the event. A man came running to our camp to surrender: he said that he had been at the fight at Ulundi, and had escaped with difficulty out of the midst of the flames: he could give no clear account of the affair, and he said that he had not ceased running until he had reached his home in this neighbourhood. Our cavalry burned Undini, Ketchwayo's old kraal, which was some fifteen miles distant, in the direction of Ekowe. They reported that in the country surrounding our camp they had passed a great many Zulus who had surrendered, that they seemed quite happy at having got away from Ketchwayo's power, and were actively engaged in rebuilding the kraals which we had burned.

On the 7th, Sir Garnet Wolseley arrived in our camp, having come on horseback from Durban; and on the next day the contingents to the Naval Brigade belonging to H.M. ships "Active" and "Shah" received orders to hold themselves in readiness to rejoin their ships. That of the "Boadicea" would have received similar directions, but it was considered advisable that it should remain a few days longer, as the presence of the men on the beach was almost indispensable for the landing of stores. A day or two subsequently we shifted our camp to the undulating ridges on the left of the road leading down to the sea. The news was brought that Dabulamanzi, who was present at the Battle of Ulundi, had ridden to the Lower Tugela, and had surrendered to Mr. Cotter, our boatswain, at Fort Tenedos. On the following day this chief arrived in our camp. He was described by those who knew him as "the best shot and the greatest scoundrel in Zululand," treacherous and cruel. I was told of an instance in which he had put to the torture a young girl belonging to his people who was discovered to have embraced Christianity, the particulars of which were extremely savage and revolting. He appeared to be a man of middle age, of medium stature, with a thin black beard and moustache, and very fat about the legs—a peculiarity, I was informed, of most of Panda's sons; he had adopted a "wide-awake" hat, the rim being lined with green, and a short shooting jacket, and he carried an English-made riding-whip, with which he beckoned to his followers, one or two in number, who very assiduously waited upon him. His principal pleasure seemed to consist in drinking, and he was so well treated in the camp that, on more than one occasion, he became greatly intoxicated.

We had extremely bad weather towards the middle of July, and I was informed—as is so usual on such occasions—that such weather had not been known since 1842. On the 18th, we were visited by Lieut. Milne, of the "Active," who arrived from Ulundi, in which battle he had been again slightly wounded; he left us the next day, to rejoin Lord Chelmsford at Durban. A friend of mine returned from Ekowe, whither he had accompanied a column which had proceeded in that direction: He informed me that the Zulus, shortly after our departure, had set all the buildings on fire, wrecked the inside of the church, and knocked holes in the walls : as the corrugated iron roof would not burn, they had stripped it off, and some of it had been thrown down a hill. But they had not in any way injured the cemetery—the crosses and graves were intact; this, however, was not from any generous motive probably, but because they are superstitious with reference to dead bodies.

A meeting took place near the Umslatoosi River, between Sir Garnet Wolseley and several important chiefs: some officers from our camp rode over to witness it. Sir Garnet told them that their country was now under the sway of the great Queen who ruled all South Africa; that she would be pleased to hear that they were happy, and that bloodshed had ceased; that she had delivered them from the cruelties of Ketchwayo; that their property would be respected, and that they might go where they liked; that they must give up all their arms and likewise the king's cattle; that in future they would have to lead peaceful lives, and that no annual assemblages would be permitted, as of yore; that the young men might marry when they liked (great signs of satisfaction were here visible among the young men, but not among the "Ring Kops," who did not seem to approve); that they were completely vanquished, and that their country would be divided into four districts, each under an Induna, and that these would be appointed when he reached Ulundi, upon which place he had four columns advancing. Sir Garnet further said that they were to scatter themselves all over the country, and communicate his words to all the remaining chiefs. Maquenda now attempted to speak, but such a clamour arose from the other chiefs, and their looks became so threatening, that he was persuaded to keep silence. Dabulamanzi, who was present, did not utter a word; but two old chiefs replied that they did not see that Ketchwayo had done any wrong, but, if the English thought so, they might kill him, as they had no objection. They were glad to hear that their rights were to be preserved, and they thanked the great Queen for it. An Induna of some note, who was expected, was not present, and, on an inquiry being made as to where he was, one of them said that he did not like beginning anything with the old moon, but the new moon would soon arrive, and then he would come in.

The day on which the Naval Brigade was to quit the Zulu country was now close at hand, and, before leaving, the officers of the "Active's" contingent invited their old friends, the officers of "the Buffs," to a farewell luncheon, which took place beneath the shade of a large tree. They were encamped with them on the Lower Tugela before the war commenced; they fought side by side with them at Inyezane; were shut up together with them during those dreary months in Fort Ekowe; and they had, finally, advanced a second time together into the Zulu country. On the morning of July 21st, the Naval Brigade was drawn up on the plain and inspected by Sir Garnet Wolseley, after which he delivered a short but eulogistic speech, and at its conclusion the following "general order" in writing was handed to Capt. Campbell:—

"*Camp at Port Durnford, July* 21*st,* 1879.

" As the Naval Brigade is now about to embark, General Sir Garnet Wolseley wishes to place on record his very high appreciation of the services it has rendered while acting on shore. The conduct of the men has been admirable, and their bearing in action in every way worthy of the service to which they belong, while they have worked

The Zulu War. 303

hard and cheerfully in those laborious duties which constitute so important a part of all military operations. In returning to their ships, they will have the satisfaction of knowing that all recollection of the Zulu War will be associated with the Naval Brigade, which has borne so distinguished a part in it.

"(By order),   G. POMEROY COLLEY,
"Major-General, Chief of the Staff."

We then marched from the ground, headed by the band of "the Buffs," and were supplied with some luncheon on the beach by the officers of the "Boadicea;" after which we said "farewell" to all our friends, and embarked in lighters towed by a steam-tug, which conveyed us to the "City of Venice" hired transport. Commodore Richards, Sir G. Wolseley, and his staff, also shortly afterwards went on board, for conveyance to Durban.

The next morning we arrived in Durban Roads, where H.M.S. "Shah" was at anchor, and her own contingent to the Naval Brigade very soon proceeded to rejoin her; some two hours subsequently, that of the "Active" embarked in lighters, which were towed to the "Shah." On nearing that ship her crew manned the rigging and cheered, and the band played several lively airs.

Early on the morning of July 24th, H.M.S. "Shah" left Durban, and it was only fitting that, before doing so, Capt. R. Bradshaw of that ship should have been waited on by a deputation of the burgesses of that town, for the purpose of presenting him with an address, and to return him thanks for the opportune aid he afforded at a very critical time. It will be remembered that H.M.S. "Shah," on her way to England from the Pacific, happened to call at St. Helena. While there, Capt. Bradshaw heard of the disaster at Isandhlwana, and its immediate consequences; upon which, having prevailed on the Governor to permit him to embark every available man of the garrison, he left for Durban with all speed, and entirely on his own responsibility, and landed between three and four hundred men from his ship, in addition to the troops which he had on board, and that at a time when, and with good reason, the greatest panic prevailed in Natal. The following article also appeared in the *Natal Mercury* on the day of our departure :—

"It is generally understood that the 'Shah'

will leave this evening with the full complement, not only of her own men, but the Naval Brigade, which was landed here last November from the 'Active.' It would be both ungracious and ungrateful to allow these gallant blue-jackets to leave Natal without some special words of thanks and recognition. The part they have borne throughout the Zulu war is one which they can look back upon with just emotions of pride and satisfaction. They have given another conspicuous example of Britain's naval pre-eminence. They have shown that the British seaman can serve his country as well upon shore as upon sea. They have, under the trying circumstances of an arduous campaign in a savage land, been cheerful, unrepining, and courageous. Their experiences have been associated in no one instance with disaster. The 'Active's' men were the first of our forces to reach the Lower Tugela. It was they who watched and kept the Border for the few weeks preceding the advance. They established and worked the pont which conveyed into Zululand the whole of the first division. They fought victoriously at Inyezane, and they were cooped up in Etshowe during the long and weary period of its isolation. After their release they joined their comrades from the 'Shah,' 'Boadicea,' and 'Tenedos' near the coast, where they too had been in action at Ginginlhovo. Then the least pleasant part of the campaign was experienced—the period of inaction, sickliness, and uncertain movement. Their only regret is that they were not allowed to march on weeks ago upon Ulundi, and had no share in that crowning episode of the war. The regret is a natural one on their part, but they have no reason to despise the record with which they take leave of Zululand. Their presence beyond the border has beyond question been a protection to Natal, and has kept in check any aggressive movement across the frontier. Their services in Natal will never be forgotten. The 'Active's' brigade was the first body of blue-jackets to land, the 'Shah' was the first batch of reinforcements to arrive, just as Cetywayo was assuming a tone of renewed and threatening defiance. Their advent spread a sense of relief and security from end to end of the colony, and enabled Lord Chelmsford to venture upon the relief of Etshowe. Whatever shortcomings may have been observed in other services, nothing can be, nothing has been, said in disparagement of the naval forces in connexion with the war. The British navy is the same as ever. As colonists, we are proud to be identified with a country which can produce a service so efficient, whose supremacy at sea is preserved by men so worthy of national respect and honour. The Brigade will be followed by as hearty a 'God speed' as ever a thankful community uttered to a body of brave defenders."

On July 29th, H.M.S. "Shah" arrived at Simon's Bay, after a splendid passage, rendered additionally enjoyable to the "Actives" by the unbounded hospitality and kindly feeling displayed towards them on every occasion by their hosts. Within a short time of the arrival of the "Shah," they rejoined their ship, receiving a most hearty reception from their old messmates, from whom they had been separated for more than eight months.

THE END.

www.ingramcontent.com/pod-product-compliance
Lightning Source LLC
Chambersburg PA
CBHW031250230426
43670CB00005B/125